VII–VIII

THE ECONOMIC HISTORY

OF THE

BALTIMORE AND OHIO RAILROAD

1827-1853

Marula
An imprint of Arcadia Publishing

The Economic History of the Baltimore and Ohio Railroad: 1827–1853
by Milton Reizenstein

A Marula Historical Reprint
Originally published in 1897

Published by Arcadia Publishing
Charleston SC

ISBN 978-0-7385-9457-6

Printed in the United States of America

For all general information contact Arcadia Publishing at:
Telephone 843-853-2070
Fax 843-853-0044
E-mail sales@arcadiapublishing.com
For customer service and orders:
Toll-Free 1-888-313-2665

Visit us on the Internet at www.arcadiapublishing.com

JOHNS HOPKINS UNIVERSITY STUDIES

IN

HISTORICAL AND POLITICAL SCIENCE

HERBERT B. ADAMS, Editor

History is past Politics and Politics are present History.—*Freeman*

FIFTEENTH SERIES

VII-VIII

THE ECONOMIC HISTORY

OF THE

BALTIMORE AND OHIO RAILROAD

1827-1853

BY MILTON REIZENSTEIN, PH. D.

Sometime Scholar in Economics, Johns Hopkins University

BALTIMORE

THE JOHNS HOPKINS PRESS

PUBLISHED MONTHLY

July-August, 1897

THE FRIEDENWALD CO. PRINTERS,
BALTIMORE.

CONTENTS.

INTRODUCTION.

It has been the intention of the writer to present a brief history of the Baltimore and Ohio Railroad from its inception in 1826 until its completion to Wheeling in January, 1853.

The monograph has been designed as a study in the economics of transportation, and stress has been laid upon the influence of the railroad in the development of the industry and commerce of the city of Baltimore, and of the agricultural, mineral and manufacturing resources of the state of Maryland. The Baltimore and Ohio having been the first great through-route railroad projected in America, has naturally an important place in the regard of the student of transportation. The beginnings of some of the present difficult railroad problems appear in the history of this road, and these have not only been treated incidentally as they appeared in connection with the legislative, financial and mechanical history of the railroad, but have been summarized in the final chapter.

The hearty thanks of the writer are due Prof. Sidney Sherwood and Dr. J. H. Hollander of the Johns Hopkins University for their valuable aid in the preparation of this monograph.

THE ECONOMIC HISTORY OF THE BALTIMORE AND OHIO RAILROAD, 1827-1853.

CHAPTER I.

ORGANIZATION OF THE BALTIMORE AND OHIO RAILWAY COMPANY.

Towards the end of the first quarter of the present century, Baltimore was confronted by the important economic problem, how to retain its rank as a prominent commercial emporium of the United States.

Other cities were drawing away from Baltimore its valuable trade with the West by introducing improved systems of transportation.

The city of New York had led the way in this particular line of enterprise by the construction of the Erie Canal—completed in 1825—extending from Albany to Buffalo. Pennsylvania had also begun to open up its resources by a judicious system of internal improvements, mainly canals, built especially for the transportation of coal.

Virginia had not been insensible to the fact that by the construction of proper canals through the valleys of the Potomac or the James rivers, a valuable commercial intercourse might be secured with the West. Ohio, too, had begun a system of internal improvements, designed to afford a channel for the outflow of its rich products as well as to provide a suitable means of ingress for foreign commodities.

It must not be supposed that Maryland had not been

alive to the importance of internal improvements or that it had taken no active steps in that direction. As early as 1784 the states of Maryland and Virginia had conjointly granted a charter to the Potomac Company, giving it power to improve the navigation of the Potomac river from tidewater to the highest practicable point on the North Branch, and to continue it thence to Cumberland by means of canals.

But this company became involved in difficulties, and a commission was appointed by the states of Maryland and Virginia in 1821 to investigate its affairs. The commission reported that the company was hopelessly insolvent, that it was unreasonable to expect that the company would ever be able to carry out the objects for which it was incorporated, and that it was best to divest the Potomac Company of its charter and adopt some more effective mode of improving the navigation of the river. This, the report continued, could be best accomplished by the construction of a regular canal outside of the river-bed, though following its ravine, and that this would be not only the most useful and durable, but incomparably the cheapest improvement. Baltimore, it was recommended, should be connected with the projected canal by a lateral branch. This report, submitted to the legislatures of Maryland and Virginia, ultimately led to the construction of the Chesapeake and Ohio Canal.

Congress had long before turned its attention to the important question of internal improvement. As early as 1806 the United States had begun the construction of the Cumberland or National Road. This road occupied the site a part of that route along which, years before, emigration and traffic over the mountains had flowed from Baltimore.

Recognizing the importance of the canal projected along the valley of the Potomac to the West, Congress in April, 1824, appropriated $30,000 for the expenses of making a survey, estimates of the probable cost, and plans for the construction of such a canal. The results, as reported by the committee of engineers appointed for the purpose, are exhibited in the following summarized table:

Sections.	Distances. Miles.	Yds.	Ascent. Descent. Feet.	Number of Locks.	Amount of Estimate.
Eastern	186	——	578	74	$8,177,081.05
Middle	70	1010	1961	246	10,028,122.86
Western	85	440	619	78	4,170,223.78
Totals	241	1450	3158	398	$22,375,427.69

The report of the commissioners appointed to inquire into the condition of the Potomac Company gave rise to the Chesapeake and Ohio Canal. The report of the engineers appointed by Congress, in the light of subsequent events, may be regarded as one of the direct causes leading to the construction of the Baltimore and Ohio Railroad. It was believed that the burden of payment would fall on the state of Maryland and the city of Baltimore rather than upon the national government. In consequence, when the enormous cost of the project became known, the enthusiasm in Baltimore for the construction of such a canal was considerably abated, and the hope of connecting Baltimore with the West by a still-water route seemed a forlorn one. Besides, there was the other very material difficulty that the scarcity of water in the Alleghanies at the high elevation over which the canal must pass would make its successful accomplishment problematic, even if the money needed could be raised. Baltimoreans, too, did not relish the idea of making Georgetown the eastern terminus of the canal, with Baltimore connected therewith by a lateral branch some fifty miles in length.

However, quick action was necessary on the part of Baltimore, for Philadelphia and New York had greatly encroached upon its trade. Turnpike roads were already behind the times. Canals, as had been shown, owing to the natural obstacles of a mountainous country, were entirely too expensive and would, besides, take too long a time to construct. Some new method of transportation must be found.

It is to Philip E. Thomas of Baltimore, more, perhaps, than to any other one man, that the credit of introducing railroads for passenger and freight traffic into the United States is due. Mr. Thomas was a Quaker merchant of Baltimore, and was also in 1826, president of the Mechanics' Bank of that city. He had been one of the commissioners on the part of the state of Maryland in the recently organized Chesapeake and Ohio Canal Company, but he had resigned that position after the futility of the scheme was shown.

With Mr. George Brown, a director in the bank of which he was president, Mr. Thomas began to study the new mode of transportation then being tried with success in England upon the Liverpool and Manchester Railway.[1] Evan Thomas, a brother of P. E. Thomas, and William Brown, a brother of George Brown, were both in England at the time and forwarded to their respective brothers in Baltimore, information relative to the new project. The conjoint study of the question by the two Baltimoreans convinced them that the railway was the method of communication with the West that Baltimore required. Having interested other prominent Baltimoreans in the plan, they determined to organize a railroad company for general traffic. This was the first company of the kind in America.

On February 12, 1827, a meeting of some twenty-five prominent citizens was held at the residence of Philip E. Thomas, to consider the best means of restoring to Baltimore that trade with the West that had been diverted. Various documents were read tending to show the great advantages which railways possessed over turnpikes and canals as a mode of transportation, and a committee was appointed to examine carefully into these advantages and into the general subject of railroads and report at the next meeting.

On the appointed evening, February 19, 1827, this com-

---

[1] This railroad was not formally opened, however, until September 15, 1830.

mittee, through its chairman, Philip E. Thomas, presented a full account of its labors. The efforts of New York and Philadelphia to divert the western trade from Baltimore were noted, as well as the plan then being proposed to connect the tide-water of the Susquehanna, by means of a canal, with the eastern extremity of the Pennsylvania state canal, in order to secure the ascending and descending trade of the Susquehanna, with the ultimate object of securing direct water communication with the Great Lakes. But no matter how important absolutely such trade might be to Baltimore, it was of minor consideration when compared with the immense commerce of the West. Baltimore was situated one hundred miles nearer the western navigable waters than was Philadelphia, the report said, and two hundred miles nearer than New York. New Orleans was pointed out as the only city which could compete with Baltimore for the western trade.

After showing at length the advantages which the canal system had in England over the same system in America, and arguing that if England with these advantages was abandoning the canal for the railroad, America might surely do so, the report pointed out that although only one[1] railway had as yet been constructed in America, the results had been very satisfactory. So far as the competition of New Orleans with Baltimore was concerned, it was stated that the western products could be delivered in Baltimore by rail at smaller expense and with less loss than at New Orleans by boat.

The value of a system of railways in the transportation of perishable food supplies was recognized in the remark

---

[1] In point of fact there were two short roads in operation in the United States at this time. The first railroad built in the United States, the one here referred to, was three miles long and extended from the granite quarries at Quincy, Mass., to the Neponset river. The second was a gravity railroad, nine miles long, extending from the coal mines at Mauch Chunk, Pa., to the Lehigh river. For full descriptions of these railroads see William H. Brown, "The History of the First Locomotives in America," ch. xii, pp. 70-71.

that if the proposed railroad were built from Baltimore to the Ohio river, an extensive market in the West would at once be opened for the fish and oysters of eastern Maryland, necessarily increasing the value of the numerous fisheries and oyster-beds of the Chesapeake Bay. This would cause a large increase of traffic upon the waters of the bay, and would open to the residents of eastern Maryland a new and highly lucrative source of wealth.

This report is to-day probably one of the best records extant of ideas in 1827 regarding railroads and their economic importance. This report of the committee was adopted, and it was resolved to apply immediately to the legislature of Maryland for an act incorporating the Baltimore and Ohio Railway Company, with all powers needed to construct a railway from the city of Baltimore to the Ohio river. A committee of twenty-five persons was appointed to apply to the legislature of Maryland for the desired act of incorporation, and another committee was appointed to examine the two railways then in operation at Mauch Chunk, Pa., and Quincy, Mass.

The report of the last-mentioned committee is dated June 12, 1827, and describes at considerable length the mode of construction of the two roads examined.[1] From their investigations the committee drew the conclusions that there would probably be no difficulty in constructing the proposed railway, but that care must be exercised in the selection of the route and the application of motive power on the road, and recommended in conclusion that a deputation be sent abroad to examine the railroads in England. Following out this advice, Jonathan Knight, an engineer, and Captain W. G. McNeill, of the U. S. Topographical Corps, were sent abroad in the autumn of 1828, and returning in the spring of the following year, reported that their examinations of the English railroads led them to approve the surveys made and route proposed for the Baltimore and Ohio Railroad.

---

[1] See note, p. 13.

In the meantime the task of drawing up a charter of incorporation for the proposed enterprise had been given to John Van Lear M'Mahon, a young lawyer of twenty-seven, who was at this time a delegate from the city of Baltimore to the Maryland legislature. The charter which he drew up was in all probability the first of its kind in America.[1] In consequence it is of enough interest to the student of transportation to merit a brief analysis.

The act to incorporate the Baltimore and Ohio Railroad Company was passed February 28, 1827. This act, which constituted the charter of the company, contained twenty-three sections. The earlier sections dealt mainly with the stock and the stockholders. They provided that the capital stock of the company should be three million dollars, in shares of one hundred dollars each, of which ten thousand shares should be reserved for subscription by the state of Maryland[2] and five thousand for subscription by the city of Baltimore[3] for the space of twelve months after the passage of the act. The remaining fifteen thousand shares were to be subscribed by individuals or corporations. As soon as ten thousand shares were subscribed the company was declared to be established with all the powers, rights and privileges conferred by the act. If more than fifteen thousand shares were subscribed, the subscription was to be reduced to that number by striking off from the largest number of shares or reducing all subscriptions to one share. If there were more than fifteen thousand different subscriptions, lots were to be drawn to determine which were to be excluded. One dollar was to be paid on every share at the time of subscribing, and the residue was to be paid in instalments; provided, however, that not more than one-third of

---

[1] Acts of Maryland Assembly, 1826, chapter 123.

[2] $500,000 subscribed under Act 1827, ch. 104; additional subscription of $3,000,000 by Act 1835, ch. 395.

[3] $500,000 subscribed under Resolutions of 1827, No. 41; additional subscription of $3,000,000 under Act of Assembly, 1835, ch. 127, and Resolutions of 1836, No. 40.

the subscription was to be demanded in any one year from the commencement of the work, nor any payment until at least 60 days' public notice of demand for payment had been given. Stock was forfeited in case any subscriber failed to pay any instalment within 60 days after it had become due.

Nine commissioners were appointed to receive the subscriptions to the capital stock, and they were to keep the books open for this purpose for at least ten successive days. The stockholders were then to elect twelve directors by ballot, and these in turn to elect a president. Each stockholder was allowed one vote for every share of stock owned by him, and voting by proxy was authorized. If the stock reserved for subscription by the state of Maryland and the city of Baltimore was not subscribed, provision was made that such stock could be disposed of by the president and directors for the benefit of the company for any sum not under its par value.

The administration of the railroad was vested entirely in the president and board of directors. They had power to appoint all the officers, engineers, agents, etc., whom they might deem necessary to transact the business of the company, with full powers of removal at will of all these employees. Further, they had power to make by-laws regulating the manner of adjusting and settling all accounts against the company, regulating the manner and evidence of transfers of the company's stock, and indeed for exercising all the powers vested in the company by the act of incorporation.

An important power was given to the president and directors by the thirteenth section, by which they were allowed to increase the capital stock of the company by the addition of as many shares as they might deem necessary, with the restriction, however, that they must not be sold below their par value. Power to borrow money and to issue mortgage bonds therefor was also granted.

The intention of the organizers of the company to build a through line from Baltimore to the Ohio river is clearly shown by the grant of power to construct such a road. The right of eminent domain was given to the president and directors, not only as regards land, but also as regards materials needed in the construction of the road. Adequate provision was, of course, made to reimburse owners for property taken by the railroad company.

There were certain restrictions put upon the powers of the company. If the road was not begun within two years from the time of the passage of the act and completed within Maryland within ten years after the time of commencement, the act was declared null and void. Full right and privilege were reserved to the citizens of Maryland to connect with the Baltimore and Ohio any other railroad leading from the main line to any other part of the state. It was provided further that whenever the Baltimore and Ohio crossed or intersected any other road or way, the railroad must be built so as not to impede the passage or transportation of persons or property along the intersected road.

Power was granted the company to place on the railroad "all machines, wagons, vehicles or carriages of any description whatsoever which they may deem necessary or proper for the purposes of transportation." The company was allowed to charge "tolls" upon goods transported over the railroad as follows: "On all goods, produce, merchandise or property of any description whatsoever transported by them from west to east, not exceeding one cent a ton per mile for toll, and three cents a ton per mile for transportation; on all goods, produce, merchandise or property of any description whatsoever transported by them from east to west, not exceeding three cents a ton per mile for tolls and three cents a ton per mile for transportation; and for the transportation of passengers, not exceeding three cents per mile for each passenger." From this quotation it is easy to see that the railroad was regarded as a new and improved kind of toll-road. This is shown also by a provision enacting that no person should travel upon or use the road of the company for transportation without permission from the officers.

As regards taxation, it was provided that the shares of the capital stock of the company should be deemed personal estate and should be exempt from the imposition of any tax or burden by the state's assent to the act of incorporation. The Court of Appeals of the state of Maryland[1] later decided that under this section of the act the property of the road of every description should be exempt from taxation.

Provision was also made in the charter for the declaration by the company of annual or semi-annual dividends out of "the nett profits arising from the resources of the said company after deducting the necessary current and probable contingent expenses," to be divided among the stockholders according to their holdings. Wilful injury done to the road was to be punished by fine or imprisonment, or both, in the discretion of the court in which the offender was tried.

Power to open subscription books, to sell stock and to organize the company was given as soon as the act was passed by the legislature of Maryland.

The citizens of Baltimore were fully alive to the local significance of a direct line of communication with the great agricultural and mineral regions of western Maryland and Ohio. It was estimated that the district which would depend mainly upon this road for the conveyance of its products contained a population of about two million persons, or nearly one-fifth of the total population of the United States at this time. Many products of the country west of the Alleghany mountains were of little value in those regions owing to the heavy expense of shipping them to a market, and it was understood that a railroad would lead to larger shipments and the trade of Baltimore be greatly increased thereby.

As a consequence, although the subscription books were open only twelve days, from March 20, 1827, until March 31, at the Mechanics' Bank in Baltimore, at the Farmers'

---

[1] Tax Cases, 12 Gill & Johnson, 117.

Branch Bank in Frederick, and at the Hagerstown Bank in Hagerstown, yet in Baltimore alone 41,788 shares were subscribed (including the 5000 shares taken by the city of Baltimore). These shares subscribed represented 22,000 individuals. Large subscriptions were also made at Hagerstown and Frederick. But as only 15,000 shares were allotted to individuals at this time, the shares were apportioned.

The Baltimore and Ohio Railroad Company was formally organized on April 23, 1827. The first board of directors elected by the stockholders consisted of Charles Carroll of Carrollton, Philip E. Thomas, William Patterson, Robert Oliver, Alexander Brown, Isaac McKim, William Lorman, George Hoffman, Thomas Ellicott, John B. Morris, Talbot Jones and William Steuart. These elected Philip E. Thomas, president of the road, and George Brown, treasurer.

The state of Virginia had confirmed the charter, March 8, 1827, and the state of Pennsylvania assented to it, February 22, 1828. The city of Baltimore was a stockholder in the railroad from its beginning, having decided by a resolution,[1] approved March 20, 1827, to take the 5000 shares of stock reserved for it by the company's charter, and provision was made for two special directors in the company to represent the interests of Baltimore.

---

[1] Session of 1827, Resolution No. 41.

CHAPTER II.

Beginning of Construction. Baltimore to Harper's Ferry (1828-1834).

Immediately after the organization of the company, preliminary surveys were begun for the location of the proposed railway. The company's engineers, Colonel S. H. Long and Jonathan Knight, were assisted by several members of the U. S. Topographical Survey. After a preliminary reconnoissance covering almost all the ground within the limits of Maryland, experimental surveys of three distinct routes were made.

The results of these surveys were communicated to the president and directors of the railroad in an exhaustive report.[1] The report confirmed the opinion that the building of the road was entirely practicable, and recommended the adoption of the route along the valley of the Patapsco, and thence in the direction of Bennett's, Bush or Linganore Creek to the Point of Rocks, where the Potomac river passes the Catoctin mountain. It was decided that the construction of the road should be at once begun along this route.

Accordingly on the Fourth of July, 1828, amid a great and enthusiastic concourse of spectators, the corner-stone of the Baltimore and Ohio Railroad was laid by the venerable Charles Carroll of Carrollton, then more than ninety years old. He is said to have remarked to one of his friends after the ceremony, "I consider this among the most important acts of my life, second only to my signing the Declaration of Independence, if even it be second to that."[1]

---

[1] "Report of the Engineers on the Reconnoissances and Surveys made in reference to the B. & O. R. R." Submitted April 5, 1828.

[2] W. P. Smith "History and Description of the Baltimore and and Ohio Railroad," p. 20.

Three days later the engineers began the definitive location of the road. In the Baltimore American for July 14, 1828, a notice was inserted by the railroad company to road-makers and bridge-builders, setting forth that from August 1 to August 11, proposals for grading and masonry on about twelve miles of the proposed road would be received at the office of the company. Newspapers of other leading cities of the country were requested to reprint this advertisement.

Grading and masonry work were first begun on 11¾ miles of road. The average cost per mile of this work was $17,000. The six miles of road nearest the city cost nearly four times as much as the remainder of this block of road, because the construction at the city end was begun at an elevation of 66 feet above mid-tide and had to be carried along at right angles to the courses of the streams. It was believed that by beginning the road at such a height and in such a direction, further extension would be practicable at a very much smaller cost. It was estimated that the cost of grading and masonry on the first forty miles would not exceed $8,000 a mile, and that with the most liberal allowance for laying the road with double tracks and completely fitting the rails for the reception of carriages and the application of motive power, the total cost per mile throughout that distance would not exceed $17,000. These estimates, it must be remembered, were made concerning an enterprise regarding the probable cost of which the data were meager and uncertain. As soon as the work on the first twelve miles was completed, proposals were received for masonry and grading for the next twelve miles, and the work was rapidly pushed on.

In the first annual report of the president of the Baltimore and Ohio Railroad Company, dated October 1, 1827, Mr. Thomas had called attention to the fact that the enterprise had been generally approved throughout the country, and more particularly in those sections of the West immediately interested in its success. He had noted the general willingness of land-holders to give, free of cost, necessary ground for the road-bed. In his second report, a year later, the president again remarked with pleasure the free cessions of land along the proposed route, as well as the fact that the right of quarrying stone had been given to the contractors. The proprietors of Ellicott's Mills—now Ellicott City—had also donated a tract of ground for a depot. There was but one unpleasant fact—a controversy with the Chesapeake and Ohio Canal Company, the railroad company's rival, in regard to the canal company's alleged pre-emption right to certain land between the Point of Rocks and Cumberland, along the Potomac river. "This controversy will probably not retard our operations in the least degree," wrote President Thomas in 1828. He was mistaken, for prolonged litigation, much expenditure of time, money and patience, and the stoppage of the extension of the railroad beyond the Point of Rocks for two years, were the consequences arising from the efforts of the canal company to check the progress of its rival.

During the year 1828 the capital stock of the company was increased from $2,000,000 to $4,000,000 by the additional subscription of $1,500,000 by individuals[1] and by a subscription of $500,000 by the state of Maryland. This last-named subscription was obtained mainly through the efforts of Mr. J. V. L. M'Mahon, and was doubtless the first time in the history of this country that a state had granted aid to a railroad corporation. The act authorizing this subscription was passed March 3, 1828 (1827, Ch. 104, Sec. 3).

Early in January, 1828, a memorial to Congress had been drawn up by the president and directors of the company, petitioning for a subscription by the United States to the company's stock. The Senate committee to which the memorial was referred reported a bill authorizing a subscription of $1,000,000. The committee of the House of Representatives also made a favorable report, but it being late in

---

[1] Original individual subscribers doubled their subscription, March 6, 1828.

the session when the committee reported, it would submit no bill. The company therefore renewed its petition at the next session of Congress in 1829, but, although the committees of both houses of Congress recommended a qualified subscription to the company, the measure failed. It was said at the time that the reason the company was unsuccessful in this application was because of the opposition of the president of the Chesapeake and Ohio Canal Company, who was at this time chairman of the committee on roads and canals in the House of Representatives.[1] But it must be remembered that there was in 1829 and 1830 considerable honest difference of opinion as to whether the United States Constitution gave power to the national government to make expenditures for objects not clearly national in character. President Jackson had strongly expressed his opposition to aiding state enterprises and schemes of internal improvement by appropriations from the central government.

From whatever source the opposition may have come, the company recognized that it must not hope for aid from the national government. By the fall of 1829 the grading and masonry upon twenty-five miles of the road had been completed, and the first rails had been laid in the early part of that year. Owing to the general advance in laborers' wages at this time, to the difficulty of procuring stone suitable for bridges and culverts, to the extensive and unexpected beds of rock and hard clay through which the roadbed had to be cut, and to the substitution of permanent stone bridges or embankments over valleys where it had been proposed to make use of wooden viaducts, the cost of these twenty-five miles had considerably exceeded the original estimate of $20,000 a mile. An injunction against the railroad company by the canal company in this year had at first compelled the railroad to cease its extension in Frederick county. The injunction was, however, partly set aside so as to allow the railroad to continue construction to the

---

[1] W. P. Smith "History and Description of the Baltimore and Ohio Railroad," p. 22.

Point of Rocks, from which point to Cumberland the ownership of the proposed routes of the two companies was in dispute.

Upon the twenty-second of May, 1830, the first division of the Baltimore and Ohio Railroad—thirteen and three-quarters miles long, from Baltimore to Ellicott's Mills—was opened for the transportation of passengers. The cars needed for general traffic, however, were not ready until early in June, but after that time the travel on the road was constant. By the first of October, 1830, the receipts were $20,012.36, although the road had only a single track and was able to transport merchandise or produce during a few months only. The freight offered for transportation was about ten times the amount which the company was able to handle.

The sight presented on that May day in 1830, upon the occasion of the opening of the first railroad worthy of the name in America, was far less imposing than that presented upon a similar occasion to-day. There were merely a number of small open carriages, much resembling the old-style stage-coaches, with wheels so constructed as to enable them to run upon the tracks. Horses were used to furnish the motive power.

The mode of locomotive power to be used upon the road was by no means decided during the first year of the railway's existence. Evan Thomas, a brother of the president, even experimented with a car which he had fitted with *sails*![1]

The railroad, being the first of its kind in the country,

---

[1] Before the experiments with the sailing car the Baltimore and Ohio Railroad made use of a "horse-power locomotive." A horse was placed in a specially constructed car and made to walk on an endless apron or belt and to communicate motion to the wheels by means of cog-wheels. The machine worked fairly well, but one day while drawing a car filled with representatives of the press, it ran into a cow, the consequence being that the whole affair tilted over and rolled down an embankment. No one was badly hurt, but the horse-power locomotive passed out of existence from that time. Brown, "The History of the First Locomotives in America," pp. 123-4.

naturally attracted much attention, and people came from considerable distances to see and travel upon this new and strange road.

The trial of the first steam locomotive on the tracks of the Baltimore and Ohio Railroad took place on August 25,[1] 1830. The locomotive, which was the first intended for railroad purposes ever built in America,[2] was the invention of Peter Cooper. It was scarcely more than a model, weighing but a single ton, and was appropriately named the "Tom Thumb." It was about the size of the hand-cars now used by workmen upon the railroad. The boiler was a small upright one, about the size of a modern kitchen boiler; its cylinder measured but three and a half inches in diameter, and its speed was gotten up by gearing. In order to secure the necessary steam pressure, a sort of bellows was used, which was worked by a pulley and cord passing over a drum on one of the car wheels. This crude machine was able to pull an open car of small dimensions from Baltimore to Ellicott's Mills, thirteen miles, in an hour and twelve minutes, and the return trip was made in fifty-seven minutes. But during a race which this engine had the same day with a similar car drawn along a parallel track by a stage horse, the band working the bellows of the engine slipped and steam-power was ignominiously beaten by horse-power.

---

[1] Or Aug. 28, 1830. Saturday, according to W. H. Brown (p. 114). This account was given to Brown by Winans, who was present upon this occasion. Cooper had tried some experimental trips with his locomotive in 1829, but it did not act as well as he had expected and desired, so he changed his plan, and after some delay made his first real experimental trip in 1830.

The Tom Thumb was built at the Mt. Clare works in 1829 (Brown, pp. 107, 108).

[2] Upon the whole subject of early locomotives and railroads in America, see the work of W. H. Brown (N. Y., Appleton & & Co., 1871), "The History of the First Locomotives in America." On Peter Cooper's "Tom Thumb" see especially pages 107 to 122 inclusive, containing a cut of the engine and an extract from a lecture delivered by Mr. H. B. Latrobe, legal counsellor of the company, before the Maryland Institute in 1868 upon the history of the Baltimore and Ohio Railroad.

Nevertheless the tiny engine was used for some time with success upon the road.

The question of granting to the company the privilege of laying tracks through the city of Baltimore from its depot on Pratt street near Poppleton to the basin or harbor, so as to facilitate the transportation of goods intended for export, directly to the vessels into which they were to be loaded, was a question which caused many heated controversies. In spite of all opposition the company prevailed, and in April, 1831,[1] the City Council gave permission to lay the proposed tracks to the basin and thence parallel to the entire water-front of the city as far as Jones Falls. At this point, the city conveyed to the company two squares of ground very favorably situated for the economical and convenient transaction of the business of the railroad.

The work of finishing the railroad as far as the Point of Rocks had meanwhile been going steadily on, and on December 1, 1831, the road was opened to Frederick, a distance of 61 miles. Frederick was not directly upon the main stem of the road, but was connected with it by a branch road 3½ miles long. On April 1, 1832, the road was opened to the Point of Rocks. Including the Frederick branch, this made 72½ miles of the road in active use after this date. With the double track, switches, sidings, etc., 130½ miles of track had now been completed.

The extension of the railroad to the Point of Rocks had an immediate effect upon that place. Several warehouses were erected; inns, dwellings and other improvements rapidly rose. The facilities for the transference of produce from the Potomac river to the railroad were ample, and the boatmen and farmers further to the west resorted more and more to the Point of Rocks as the most convenient spot from which to reach the Baltimore market.[2] It was stated also that every species of agricultural product, lime,

---

[1] By act of Baltimore City Council, Session of 1831, Ordinance No. 18. Approved April 4, 1831.

[2] Sixth Annual Report of the B. & O. R. R. Co. (1832), p. 4.

timber of various kinds, and even paving-stones had been brought to Baltimore with profit to those making use of the road. In return (although at an enhanced toll, yet still with equally profitable results) plaster of paris, coal, boards, bricks and scrap iron had been sent into the interior. The existence of the road had also brought into use articles, in the sparsely settled country through which the railroad passed, which had before been valueless to their possessors. Forests and quarries hitherto useless became sources of new profit to the owners.

The mode of construction of the road to the Point of Rocks was various and was in the nature of a series of experiments.[1] The combination of the iron rail on granite, the wood and iron rail on stone blocks, the wood and iron rail supported by broken stone, the same supported by longitudinal ground-sills instead of broken stone, the log rail formed of trunks of trees worked to a surface on one side to receive the iron and supported by wooden sleepers, and the wrought-iron rails in use on the English railroads, had all been tried and formed at this time parts of the work. In general, stone, wherever easily obtainable, had been preferred to wood for supporting the rails, because of its supposed greater durability, but subsequent experience proved that this preference was without good reason.

By this time any question as to the suitability of the railway as a mode of transporting persons and merchandise was practically settled by the successful operation of this road. The important question to settle was the kind of locomotive needed. It was evident that horses would not suffice for the long distances and the heavy traffic, and that steam must be employed. It was thought that the English locomotives were not adapted to this American railway, with its steep grades and sharp curves—some of them not more than 400 feet in radius. The Peter Cooper engine was

---

[1] Almost total reconstruction of this portion of the railroad was necessary within 10 years.

altogether inadequate. It was determined to advertise for American locomotives.

On January 4, 1831, the company published a notice offering $4,000 for the most approved engine which should be delivered for trial upon the road on or before June 1 of the same year, and offering $3,500 for the engine adjudged the next best. It was specified, among other things, that these engines must burn coke or coal; must consume their own smoke; must not exceed three and a half tons in weight; be capable of regularly drawing on a level road fifteen tons fifteen miles per hour; steam pressure not to be over 100 pounds per square inch; company to have the right to test boilers, fire-tubes, cylinders, etc.; each engine to be provided with two safety valves, one of them out of reach and control of the engineer; engine and boiler to be supported on springs and to rest on four wheels, with the top of the chimney not more than twelve feet from the ground, and to be fitted with a mercurial gauge with index to show the steam pressure above fifty pounds per square inch and constructed to blow out at 120 pounds, etc., etc.

When the time specified for the trial had arrived, three locomotives were submitted for competition. But one, called "The York," (from its having been built at York, Pa.), stood the test. It had been built by Davis and Gartner and weighed 3½ tons. It was mounted on wheels such as those on the common cars, thirty inches in diameter, and ordinarily made the trip between Baltimore and Ellicott's Mills, drawing four cars, making up a gross weight of 14 tons, in one hour. On straight parts of the road and for short distances it had reached the speed of thirty miles an hour. It easily ran over curves as small as 400 feet radius, but owing to its light weight was of little use when heavy grades were to be ascended. The success of this engine and the satisfaction that it gave in its regular use after its trial led President Thomas to remark in his annual report in 1832 that the engine was but "as the commencement of a series of experiments which will even more fully than has yet been done, prove the adaptation of steam and railroads to every part of our country and for all purposes of trade and travel." During 1832 a number of other mechanics and inventors were engaged in the construction of locomotive engines. Davis and Gartner placed a second engine, the "Atlantic," upon the rails of the Baltimore and Ohio Railroad during that year, and this engine proved quite as successful as their first one.

In 1832 the controversy so long pending between the Chesapeake and Ohio Canal Company and the Baltimore and Ohio Railroad Company came to a final settlement. The Court of Appeals by a vote of three judges to two—the sixth judge of the court being ill and not voting—reversed the decision of the Chancery Court of Maryland and sustained the contention of the canal company in its claim to a prior right of way between the Point of Rocks and Harper's Ferry. The railroad company was not to appropriate or use the land between these points until the canal company had laid out its route. It was believed that the canal company would probably use so much of the narrow available space between these points as to exclude the railroad.

The railroad company, beaten in the courts, had still several alternatives left. It might continue the road alongside the canal between the two points in question upon such ground as the canal company might leave vacant; it might cross the Potomac river at the Point of Rocks and continue its line along the Virginia shore of the river; it might tunnel through the mountain spurs; finally, it might succeed in procuring permission from the canal company to construct jointly the two works from the Point of Rocks to Harper's Ferry.

The last-named plan was the first one tried. While the case had still been in the Chancery Court, the chief engineers of the two companies, acting as commissioners of the court, had reported that from surveys made by them the plan was feasible and that its execution would involve an increased cost of about $7,000 to each company. In the proposition submitted by the railroad company to the canal company, the former offered to bear the whole increased expense of the undertaking ($14,000) if the canal company would permit the proposed joint construction. This offer the canal company declined, on the ground that it might work harm to the canal.

The legislature of Maryland now intervened. Both enterprises were of too much value to the state and to the country at large to permit the usefulness of either to be impaired by friction between them. A resolution was first passed by both houses of the legislature urging an accommodating spirit upon the canal company towards the railroad company and a modification of the plan of the canal so as to permit the joint construction of both enterprises. In answer to this appeal the railroad company offered to construct the canal at the price at which it had been put under contract, to complete it by a fixed date, to guarantee it to stand for five years, and to keep it in thorough repair during that time. To this offer the canal company proposed that the railroad company should devote the unexpended portion of its capital to the completion of the canal to Cumberland and abandon for the time all idea of continuing the railroad beyond the Point of Rocks.

The railroad immediately rejected this offer as unreasonable. Things were, therefore, again at a standstill. In the legislative session of 1832-33 the Committee on Internal Improvements in the House of Delegates was directed to examine the region in question and to report upon the feasibility of joint construction of the two works. This report was so hostile to the canal company that relations became all the more strained. Matters looked very dark for the extension of the railroad in Maryland, when it was proposed to appoint a joint committee of the two branches of the legislature for the purpose of harmonizing the differences between the two companies without attempting to force concessions.

The proposition was favorably received, the committee

was organized, and investigations were made with the co-operation of the companies interested. A report, embodying a compromise, was submitted, and a law, practically the same as the compromise report, was passed by the legislature, March 22, 1833.

By this law the consent of the canal company to the joint construction of the railroad with the canal through the region between the Point of Rocks and Harper's Ferry was recorded. It was provided, too, that when completed to Harper's Ferry the railroad was to subscribe for 2,500 shares of the stock of the canal company, and that the railroad company was to be allowed to begin the construction of its road at the Point of Rocks at any time after May 10, 1833. The canal company was bound to prepare the road-bed through the passes of the Point of Rocks for one hundred thousand dollars and to bear the expense of any additional cost of grading. The width of the canal was to be maintained at fifty feet, but if the railroad became impracticable at any point in the passes with the canal fifty feet wide, its width might be contracted to forty feet, if the commissioners—provided for in a subsequent part of the law—deemed necessary. The canal company was given the right to grade the road-bed within a limited time, preserving a greater width for the canal than forty feet if it differed in opinion with the commissioners.

The railroad, on the other hand, was to have a breadth of not less than twenty feet through the passes of the Point of Rocks, and a curvature of not less than 400 feet radius, and a grade not greater than thirty feet to the mile. To determine points at issue between the two companies, as to the construction of the road, a board of commissioners was to be created, composed of three engineers, one to be chosen by the canal company, one by the railroad company, and the third by the President of the United States. These commissioners were to determine the damages payable by the railroad company to the canal company for any interruption—during the construction or in consequence of it—

of the use of any part of the canal. It was provided, too, that a fence was to be erected, under the direction of the commissioners, between the two works, sufficient to secure the horses used on the canal from accidents from the passage of the locomotives. It was found, however, that a fence was out of the question, because it would act as a barrier to the free flow of melted snow and mountain washings which would thus accumulate and flood the tracks. Therefore the railroad company was obliged to use horses to draw its cars between the Point of Rocks and Harper's Ferry until the objectionable clause was repealed.

Under this compromise act the railroad company paid the canal company $266,000 in monthly instalments, which amount President Thomas of the Baltimore and Ohio said that he did not consider more than sufficient fully to cover, as was intended, the cost of construction of those portions of the railroad which the canal company had undertaken to build, as well as to indemnify it for the loss and damage to which the canal company, during the period of construction, must necessarily be subject. Besides it was important for the railroad to reach Harper's Ferry as soon as possible.[1] Among the chief reasons for this was, that at that point was the northern terminus of the Winchester and Potomac Railroad, which bade fair to transfer to the Baltimore and Ohio Railroad at Harper's Ferry, the passengers and produce gathered along its thirty miles of route in Virginia. Winchester, itself a thriving town, would be brought thus into close connection with Baltimore, probably to the mutual advantage of the two places.

Persons who had invested their money in the railroad were evidently becoming impatient for some returns, for President Thomas in his report in 1833 remarked that the board of directors saw that much was still to be done before those pecuniary advantages originally anticipated could be realized to the stockholders. Indeed, instead of having

---

[1] Seventh Annual Report of the B. O. R. R. Co., p. 5 (1833).

money to distribute among the stockholders, the need of funds to continue the construction of the railroad was so urgent that at the session of the Maryland legislature of 1833 the state treasurer was authorized to pay to the company the whole of the state's subscription to the stock. The Mayor and City Council of Baltimore also having passed an ordinance to the same effect as regarded the city's shares of stock, the company found itself in possession of the necessary resources to continue the road to Harper's Ferry. The canal company having built the railroad through the passes of the Point of Rocks, and the railroad company, with the necessary additions to its resources, having been able to continue the construction at the point the canal company had left it, the whole route to Wager's Bridge, a point opposite Harper's Ferry on the Maryland side of the Potomac, was opened on December 1, 1834. Here the further progress of the railroad ceased until the summer of 1836, when surveys for the extension of the road westward were begun.

Although there was a general decline in the business of the country at large during 1834, yet there was a steady increase in the business of the Baltimore and Ohio Railroad. To this the president of the railroad calls attention in his report for that year,[1] saying that this increase was not attributable to the augmentation of business from any one place, but due rather to the multiplication of places with which trade was carried on by means of the railroad. The expenses of the railroad had also been reduced by the economical employment of steam power.

As the Baltimore and Ohio Railroad was the foremost of the railroads in America, it had to solve many problems in the technique of railroading during the early years of its existence, and many improvements in locomotives, rolling stock and road-building were introduced by the engineers and mechanics of the road.

Beginning in 1830, experiments were made to test the

---

[1] Eighth Annual Report of the B. & O. R. R. Co. (1834), p. 12.

comparative resistance of cars equipped with the Winans anti-friction boxes and those with hardened steel journals and chilled bearings. The friction on a straight, level road was found to amount to $\frac{1}{240}$ of the load in the case of the latter equipment and to $\frac{1}{400}$ part of the load with the Winans invention. The combined cylindrical and conical car wheels, which allowed cars to go safely around sharp curves of a small radius, and which were especially useful in turning the corners of city streets, were the invention of Jonathan Knight, then chief engineer of the road.[1] When locomotives took the place of horse-power, the light coach wheels were replaced by cast-iron wheels, to the perfection of which Ross Winans, John Elgar, Jonathan Knight and Phineas Davis all contributed. Thousands of these cast-iron wheels were made at Ross Winans' shops, not only for American roads, but also for export for German and Swiss roads, where they were used up to 1851.

Next to the improvements in steam locomotives during these years the most striking development was probably that made in the cars. These, built originally very like the stage-coaches of the day and mounted on four light cast-iron wheels, were gradually changed and improved, owing to the demands for greater steadiness and convenience in coaches, until in his report dated October 1, 1833, the superintendent, Ross Winans, announced that he was building three car bodies to form one coach on eight wheels to carry sixty passengers. This was the beginning of the modern eight-wheel car.[2] Soon after, eight-wheel cars were used through-

---

[1] The credit for this invention was claimed by James Stimpson, an inventor, originally from Massachusetts, who was also the inventor of jointed axles for railroad cars, and who claimed that he had invented the mode of placing rails so that cars could with safety go around the small curves of city streets. James Stimpson had a long series of suits in the courts in order to protect his inventions, some of which suits he won.

[2] Winans patented the eight-wheel car, but the courts decided adversely to his claim, on the ground of prior use, in that two four-wheel cars connected by a pole and "bolster" (the use of which on the B. & O. to carry 40-foot timber stringers had sug-

out the line for both passenger and freight traffic, and special cars were provided for baggage, which had before this time been carried in racks upon the tops of the coaches.

In September, 1832, steel springs were first placed upon the locomotive "York" and its tender, which experiment was so successful that springs of steel were also put on some freight cars with equal success. By the summer of 1833 it was thought advisable for the company to begin the manufacture of its own engines and to keep them in repair, rather than have all these things done by contract, as had theretofore been the case. Accordingly the company began to erect shops in Baltimore where the great Mount Clare works now stand. Up to July, 1834, the company had had but three locomotives, the "York," the "Atlantic," and the "Franklin." Many cars, especially freight cars, were still drawn by horse or mule power. By the fall of 1834 five more locomotives, all American built—the "Traveller," "Arabian,"[1] "Mercury," "Antelope" and "American," the last two having been built in Baltimore—were put upon the road. Eight more locomotives had been ordered and were then under contract.

---

gested the idea of an eight-wheel car to Winans) had already been generally used, as well as a similar arrangement for transporting large blocks of granite at Quincy, Mass. Cf. Address of Prest. Mendes Cohen before American Society of Civil Engineers, 1892, p. 551 of the "Proceedings," etc.

[1] This was the type of the famous "Grasshopper engine."

CHAPTER III.

EXTENSION. HARPER'S FERRY TO CUMBERLAND.
(1834-1842.)

By the compromise with the Chesapeake and Ohio Canal Company the Baltimore and Ohio Railroad Company had agreed not to continue its road along the banks of the Potomac beyond Harper's Ferry until the canal should be finished to Cumberland, provided that this were done within the time allowed by the charter of the canal company. The route to the West through Virginia was open to the railroad, but the president and directors did not at this time deem it advisable to extend their railroad through that state.

The eight annual report of the railroad (1834) announced that in the opinion of the board of directors " the immediate interest of the stockholders as well as of the city of Baltimore and the state of which Baltimore is the heart and emporium, now lies in the completion of the Chesapeake and Ohio Canal to Cumberland. For the present, therefore, the board would not think of making the railroad parallel to the canal, even if it had the power, but taking up the route where the canal terminates at Cumberland, would push the railroad across the mountains upon the trace originally intended for it and to the point of its original destination. The two enterprises would then be united in interest, instead of hostile, and jointly afford the desired communication from Baltimore to the West."[1] This plan was, however, not carried out.

In the last report issued by Philip E. Thomas as president of the railroad company,[2] attention is called to the fact that in spite of many obstacles the business of the road had

---

[1] Eight Annual Report B. & O. R. R. Co. (1834), pp. 14-15.
[2] Ninth Annual Report B. & O. R. R. Co. (1835), p. 4.

increased during the fiscal year ending October 1, 1835. Acknowledgment is made of the liberal policy of those Baltimore merchants to whom the new trade of the interior of the state and the West generally had been directed, and of their title to the thanks of the railroad company and the community generally for the efforts they had made to render the Baltimore market popular and attractive in those sections of the country where hitherto it had been but little known.

This was a time of considerable activity in railroad construction. The Baltimore and Port Deposit Railroad when completed would connect with a system of railroads running from Port Deposit through Philadelphia to New York, giving a through route from that city to Washington, or from New York through Baltimore and via the Winchester and Potomac Railroad—with which the Baltimore and Ohio Railroad was now practically connected—to Winchester, situated in the heart of Virginia, about 115 miles from Baltimore. The town of Chambersburg in Pennsylvania desired to secure connection with these arteries of commerce and asked for an examination of the country between that place and the terminus of the Baltimore and Ohio Railroad at Harper's Ferry. In accordance with this request, Benjamin H. Latrobe, later the chief engineer of the Baltimore and Ohio Railroad, was detailed for the duty. He reported that a railroad 45 miles long would connect the two points, and that one inclined plane with stationary power would be necessary. The cost of such a road he estimated at about $10,000 per mile. However, nothing more was done in regard to this proposed road at this time.

The cities of Pittsburgh and Wheeling were both desirous of being connected with Cumberland by railroad. At the request of the people of Wheeling, Jonathan Knight, the chief engineer of the Baltimore and Ohio Railroad, made a reconnoissance between these points in the summer of 1835. He reported that the mountains between Cumberland and the western waters could be passed by locomotives and their trains without the use of stationary power or inclined planes, and that a road to Pittsburgh was just as practicable as one to Wheeling. The directors of the Baltimore and Ohio Railroad were of the opinion that the means by which these proposed roads were to be constructed ought to come from all those interested in the completion of the work, since such a line would be for their mutual advantage. Therefore it was proposed that the state of Maryland, the city of Baltimore and individual subscribers should furnish the means to build the railroad from Harper's Ferry to Cumberland, and that Pittsburgh and Wheeling should supply the funds necessary for the construction of their respective branches from Cumberland. The total expense of building these proposed roads was roughly estimated at $4,600,000. Some time before, the city of Wheeling had tendered a subscription of $500,000 for this purpose. This plan was not immediately carried out, although the railroad was completed to Wheeling in 1853, and later on to Pittsburgh via the Pittsburgh and Connellsville Railroad, a branch of the Baltimore and Ohio. In both cases aid for the construction of the road came from the city to which the railroad was extended.

At the December session of the Maryland legislature of 1835-36 the board of directors of the railroad asked for aid from the state in order to complete the railroad to Pittsburgh and to Wheeling, and at about the same time a similar application was made to the Mayor and City Council of Baltimore. The city responded by resolving to subscribe the sum of three million dollars ($3,000,000) to the capital stock of the company whenever the legal difficulties[1] which prevented at that time the extension of the railroad in an unbroken line from Harper's Ferry to the western waters should be removed. In the legislature the bill to aid the railroad was opposed and postponed until the extra May session. In the meantime a largely attended convention

[1] Agreement with the Chesapeake and Ohio Canal Company.

was held in Baltimore, to which delegates from Pittsburgh and Wheeling came, and in which various subjects connected with the internal improvements of the state were fully discussed.

One result of this convention was that at the May session of the legislature a law[1] was passed, containing among other subscriptions for the furtherance of internal improvements in Maryland, one of three million dollars ($3,000,000) to the capital stock of the Baltimore and Ohio Railroad. The same law released the company from the restrictions that prevented the extension of the railroad westward from Harper's Ferry, and thereby enabled it to comply with the condition annexed to the subscription by the Mayor and City Council of Baltimore. But before the law could go into effect the assent of both the Chesapeake and Ohio Canal Company and the Baltimore and Ohio Railroad Company was necessary. The consent of the railroad company was, of course, immediately forthcoming at a general meeting of the stockholders, July 18, 1836. Not so, however, with regard to the canal company. Old jealousies and contentions had not been forgotten and the canal company took no action in the matter. The directors of the railroad company were authorized by the stockholders to endeavor to secure the canal company's assent to the law. The directors of the railroad finally succeeded by means of a written agreement in removing the apprehensions of the canal company that any of the provisions of the law regarding the joint construction of the railroad and the canal would, if carried into operation, materially impair the permanence or usefulness of the canal, and after considerable delay the law went into effect. The subscription of the state treasurer for 30,000 shares was received September 23, 1836, and that of the Mayor of Baltimore, September 27, 1836.

The subscription of $3,000,000 by the state was made to depend upon certain important conditions. The stockhold-

---

[1] Acts of 1835, ch. 395. Passed June 4, 1836.

ers of the railroad company in general meeting were to bind the company in a written agreement to guarantee to the state of Maryland after the expiration of three years from the payment by the state of each of the instalments on the stock subscribed, the payment from that time on, out of the profits of the company, of six per cent per annum, payable semi-annually, on the amount of the money paid to the company, until the clear annual profits of the railroad should be more than sufficient to discharge the interest payable to the state of Maryland, and adequate, besides, to a dividend of six per cent per annum among its stockholders. Thereafter the state was to receive upon the stock it held a perpetual dividend of six per cent per annum out of the profits of the company as declared from time to time, and no more, and all the profits above six per cent per annum were to be distributed among the other stockholders according to their interests in the company. In consideration of this guarantee of interest to the state, the railroad company was authorized to increase the charge for transportation of passengers to any amount not exceeding one cent per mile for each person, in addition to the charge already authorized to be made by the company, making the aggregate four cents per person per mile.

The guarantee required of the stockholders was given at a general meeting held in Baltimore, July 18, 1836.[1]

---

[1] This "preferred stock" has had an interesting history. The state of Maryland paid its subscription in 5 per cent sterling bonds, which could not be sold advantageously for many years. At the time of the receipt of the bonds the company charged itself on its books with the bonds at their face value, $3,200,000. The account stood in that form until September 30, 1853, when it was closed with an entry of $3,000,000 to "preferred stock" and the transfer of $200,000 to the account of "Interest west of Cumberland." This "preferred stock" was sold by the state of Maryland (Md. Laws, 1842, ch. 301), and eventually about $1,000,000 worth came into the possession of the Johns Hopkins University. Six per cent interest was paid on this stock until the half-year ending June 30, 1896, when further payment was refused. This has led to the case now in the Circuit Court of the United States for the District of Maryland (The Mercantile Trust Company vs. The Balti-

The president's report for 1836 reveals the unsatisfactory financial condition of the road. The following table of rates is quoted to show, by comparison with charges authorized by the laws of other states, that the rates on the Baltimore and Ohio as fixed by law were too low.

Railroads.		Persons per mile.	Goods per ton per mile.
Petersburg		5 cents.	10 cents.
Winchester and Potomac		6	7
Portsmouth and Roanoke		6	8
Boston and Providence		5	10
Boston and Lowell		3½	7
Mohawk and Hudson		5	8
Baltimore and Ohio	Old law	3	Eastwardly 4
	New law	4	Westwardly 6

In the absence of competition other than the Chesapeake and Ohio Canal, the railroad might profitably have raised its rates much higher had there been no legal restriction. As it was, not only was no dividend declared during the fiscal year ending October 1, 1836, but the six million dollars subscription of the city and state not having been available, an instalment of five dollars per share of stock had to be called for. The revenues had fallen off—a sign portentous of the crisis of 1837—and the expenditures had been heavy. The cost of constructing the viaduct over the Potomac river at Harper's Ferry was very great, and a large and constant outlay was required for new engines and cars. Extensive repairs had been necessary, for the railroad as originally constructed was largely experimental and many parts of it were ill calculated to stand the strain of the heavy

more and Ohio Railroad Company et al. in re Johns Hopkins University, petitioner), the point of which is to decide whether the interest must be paid or whether the provisions of the law of 1836 have been complied with and the railroad company released from interest payments on this stock unless that interest is earned on the whole capital stock of the railroad.

traffic for which it soon began to be used. Therefore the accruing revenue for these purposes was used in anticipation of the payments on instalments of stock. In fact the above instalment of $5 had been called for in order to repay money borrowed. To offset this, the amount that had been applied to construction of the main stem, and not to general expenses other than construction, was to be divided by the number of shares of stock of the main stem and each share credited with its proportion as so much paid in. It was contended in this report that the reason that the Baltimore and Ohio did not pay was because it was not completed. All the railroads in the country that had been completed were paying very well, it was claimed.

The legislature at its extra session in May, 1836, had passed another law of importance to the railroad. By this act the company was released from its obligation to erect a board fence between the railroad and the canal from the Point of Rocks to Harper's Ferry as a condition precedent to the use of steam between the two places, provided that the railroad company would first tender to the canal company the price of a "post and rail fence" for that distance. As the construction and existence of such a fence had been impracticable, the railroad company had been compelled to use horse and mule-power between these points at a great expense.

The tenth annual report also gives an account of reconnoissances and surveys of the route along the Potomac westward from Harper's Ferry and of the country west of Cumberland as far as Wheeling. Mention is also made of an extension by the Maryland legislature of the time allowed for the completion of the main stem of the railroad within the state from July 4, 1838—the time fixed by the act of incorporation—to July 4, 1843.[1]

Louis McLane assumed his duties as president of the Baltimore and Ohio Railroad in April, 1837, and his first

---

[1] By acts of 1835, ch. 245. Passed March 28, 1836.

report appeared the following October. That the year was a critical one is easily read in and between the lines of this report. The cost of constructing the main stem had exceeded the capital paid in by $202,968.94. This had been supplied by using $61,200[1] of a million dollar loan negotiated by the railroad company and payable January 1, 1854, and by notes of the company issued to the amount of $141,768.94. The last-named amount was to be paid by the two instalments on the capital stock which were due September 30 and October 31, 1837, amounting together to $150,000.

At a meeting of the directors held in July, 1837, a committee was appointed consisting of the president and five members to investigate fully the affairs of the company, to inquire into the practicability of reducing expenditures and of providing an efficient and economical organization in all departments. It was clear that the road must be in a large measure completely and promptly rebuilt in a more thorough manner than it had been built at first. It was decided that for this reconstruction the portion of the capital yet unpaid would furnish the readiest and most certain resource. In the then existing condition of the company and the money market it was felt that proper reliance could not be placed upon loans, even if they could be obtained at the heavy rates of interest then current. The revenue could thus be devoted to paying a dividend. This cautious policy the company followed.

In the fall of 1837 the sum of $15 was still due upon each share of the stock, making in the aggregate $450,000, and this was devoted to the reconstruction of the road. The stockholders were called upon to pay this sum in instalments of $2.50 each in August, September, October and November, 1838, and in January and March, 1839, respectively. During 1838 the reduction-of-expenses policy was carried out with

[1] This sum was part of the $1,000,000 loan of 1834 made by the Baltimore and Ohio to purchase stock in the Washington Branch, and represented the proceeds of the loan not required for the purpose. It was the first bond issue of the company.

success, so that the income of the road exceeded the expenditures by more than $7,000. During this year also the company made active efforts to secure the necessary funds and legislation to extend the railroad farther westward.

In the course of the year B. H. Latrobe made a full and careful report of the surveys of the country between Harper's Ferry and Pittsburgh and Wheeling. He expressed the opinion that it was practicable to locate a satisfactory route to the Ohio river, embracing both cities, at the maximum gradient of 66 feet per mile, and that with a single track of the best construction from Cumberland to both these points the whole of the work from Harper's Ferry ought not to exceed $9,500,000.

In order to extend the road to Wheeling it was necessary to secure the extension of the time during which the railroad company might have the right to build its road through Virginia. By the original permission which Virginia had given (by the confirmation of the Maryland act of incorporation of 1827), the time allowed the railroad to build in Virginia expired in July, 1838. After considerable difficulty the passage of a law[1] was obtained in 1838 extending the time five years. But this law provided that the extension of time was granted only upon condition that the road be carried into Virginia at Harper's Ferry and thence continued through that state to a point about five and a half miles below Cumberland. It was provided, too, that Wheeling was to be one of the termini of the road. Besides a subscription of $302,100[2] which had been made by the State of Virginia a short time before, this law authorized an additional subscription by the state of $1,058,420—two-fifths of the estimated cost of so much of the road as was required to be built in Virginia between Harper's Ferry and Cumberland. By this law the railroad company was compelled either to abandon altogether the extension of the

[1] Acts of Virginia Assembly, 1838, ch. 159. Passed April 2, 1838.

[2] Acts of Virginia Assembly, 1836, ch. 136. Passed March 28, 1837.

road to Wheeling or to leave the State of Maryland for nearly the entire distance between Harper's Ferry and Cumberland.

The validity of the act of the Virginia legislature depended upon its acceptance by the stockholders of the railroad, including the state of Maryland. Preparatory to accepting the act it was imperative that it should first be determined whether a crossing at Harper's Ferry into Virginia was practicable. There were two possible ways for the railroad to cross the Potomac river at this point: either to secure permission from the Winchester and Potomac Railroad Company to occupy and make use of about six miles of its road, or to secure permission from the national government to occupy a part of the government property at Harper's Ferry. The Winchester and Potomac Railroad Company refused permission to make use of its road, but in November, 1838, an agreement was made with the Secretary of War at Washington whereby the use of the government land was granted to the railroad company. At a meeting of the stockholders, November 13, 1838, at which 88,871 shares of stock were represented, the Virginia law was accepted. The principal reason which induced the stockholders to build their railroad outside of Maryland for nearly a hundred miles was that Wheeling was regarded at that time as an indispensable terminus of the road. Other considerations also operated, such as the trade which was expected to come from the fertile valleys of the regions bordering on the tributaries of the Potomac river; the avoidance of any collision with the Chesapeake and Ohio Canal, then far advanced in its construction; and finally, the much greater economy in constructing the railroad through Virginia.

From the surveys and estimates that had been made, it was calculated that the difference between the cost of constructing the road through Virginia and through Maryland would be not less than $2,083,917 in autual outlay in money, and really equal to not less than $2,625,400 in actual equivalent capital. When to this there was added the sum of

$2,358,420, the joint contributions of the state of Virginia and the city of Wheeling—all of which would have necessarily been relinquished had the stockholders voted to abandon the idea of constructing the railroad in Virginia—the difference in favor of following the Virginia route amounted to $4,983,420 in actual and equivalent capital. With these subscriptions from Wheeling and Virginia just mentioned, the apparent resources of the company to complete the railroad to Pittsburgh and Wheeling were as follows:

Subscription by state of Maryland......	$3,000,000
Subscription by city of Baltimore......	3,000,000
Subscription by state of Virginia.......	302,100[1]
Additional subscription by state of Va..	1,058,420[1]
Subscription by the city of Wheeling...	1,000,000
	$8,360,520

Estimated cost of completing the road..	$9,500,000
Amount subscribed	8,360,520
Amount still required	$1,139,480

The subscription of the city of Baltimore was limited by the terms of the ordinance authorizing it to the construction of the railroad between Harper's Ferry and Cumberland. It was payable in cash at the rate of not more than $1,000,000 per year. To raise this sum the city commissioners of finance were authorized to issue city stock paying six per cent interest. But the condition of the money market in 1838, 1839 and 1840 was such as to render it impossible to put these stocks on the market at par. Therefore, instead of trying to float this large amount of city securities, the city commissioners of finance at first borrowed the money needed for the instalments called for by the railroad directly from the banks of Baltimore, and in order to meet the inter-

[1] Repealed by acts of Virginia Assembly, 1846, ch. 99, sec. 3.

est on the loans the City Council levied a direct tax to cover the amount of interest for the first year. These loans were made by the banks upon deposits of city stock as security.

Later on the stringency in the money market led to a very interesting but not altogether successful financial scheme. At a meeting of the directors of the company held in the autumn of 1839 it was decided that something must be done to make the subscription of Baltimore immediately available at the par value of the six per cent city stock. Therefore it was determined to offer to contractors for their work and to the owners of land in payment for the right of way, certificates, payable when presented in sums of $100, in Baltimore City six per cent stock at par. That entire confidence might be felt in these certificates the requisite amount of city stock was to be received by the company simultaneously with each issue of certificates, and be immediately vested in two commissioners in trust for the holders of the certificates. These certificates did not promise to pay money, nor were they promissory at all in character. They conferred an absolute authority for the transfer of city stock when presented in the requisite amounts, and when this stock was received, the obligation for which the certificates had been received in satisfaction was finally cancelled. They were therefore not paper money, although they might and did circulate as currency.

The scheme was at first successful. The contractors and land-owners to whom they were offered accepted them without demur. They in turn gave them to their workmen in return for labor. Here they were again accepted and so passed on into general circulation and floated the city stocks for a while at par. By September, 1840, the payments made through this medium amounted to $515,000. The number of certificates issued and their denominations were as follows: 100 of $100 each, 6,800 of $5 each, 13,000 of $3 each, 39,000 of $2 each and 354,000 of $1 each. By the autumn of 1840 only the 100 certificates for $100 each had been redeemed in city stock. The saving of interest to the city due to the amount of the certificates kept in circulation was considerable. In addition to the amount paid by certificates, the payments by the direct delivery of the city stock amounted by September 30, 1840, to $138,877.47. The certificates, being fundable in city stock at par not worth that sum in the market, soon depreciated in value and much injury was done to the workmen holding these certificates, who were compelled to receive them at par in payment for their labor.[1] A potent factor in depreciating these certificates was a resolution passed by the City Council of Baltimore in 1842 (Resolution No. 52) repealing the ordinances of February, 1841, allowing the certificates to be received in payment of taxes and city dues.

By this means the extension of the railroad was continued during a time when many other works of internal improvement throughout the country were partially or wholly suspended. The credit of the state also was preserved from probable impairment, for the Virginia subscriptions, afterwards repealed, were not available, and before the certificate scheme had been conceived the six per cent city stock had not been regarded as negotiable. Therefore the $3,000,000 subscription of the state of Maryland had been looked to as the means whereby the construction of the railroad was to be carried on. This subscription of $3,000,000 by the state had originally been payable to the company in cash to be raised by the sale of state currency bonds bearing interest at six per cent. These bonds were to be offered for sale first in Europe before being put upon any other market. When the attempt was made to put these bonds upon the European market the state's commissioner in Europe reported that it was impracticable to do so, and wrote that sterling, instead of currency bonds, might prove more salable. The legislature of Maryland therefore changed the bonds to sterling bonds, bearing interest at five per cent and payable, principal and interest, in London. In order to provide for the interest for three years, an amount

[1] See contemporary Baltimore newspapers and broadsides.

of bonds equal to $3,200,000 was issued and delivered directly to the railroad company in full payment of the state's subscription, the company giving the requisite guarantee for the payment of interest.

Inquiries having revealed the fact that these bonds could not advantageously be disposed of either in New York or Philadelphia, President McLane went to London to endeavor to place the bonds on the European market as profitably as possible. But by the time the bonds could be prepared and forwarded to London an unfavorable change had taken place in the European market so far as American securities were concerned. Such securities had accumulated in unprecedented quantities and a general depression in their value had taken place. Many causes had combined to weaken confidence in American credit, one of the most important, of course, being the repudiation of their debts by a number of American states and the suspension of interest payments upon their public debts by others—the state of Maryland being in the latter class. The knowledge that there would be forced sales of bonds like those of the state of Maryland at extremely low rates, rendered the sale of those belonging to the company absolutely impossible, except at rates ruinous to the interests of the company and extremely injurious to the credit of the state. For these reasons President McLane would not put the bonds upon the market. Instead, an arrangement was made with the house of Baring Brothers & Company of London by which that house agreed to advance such sums as loans to the company as it might require, for which the state bonds were deposited as security. The bonds were to be put upon the market, from time to time, in both Europe and America, in such amounts as the market might seem able to bear, upon terms favorable to the credit of the state and the interests of the railroad company. The necessity for such a loan was obviated, however, for the time by the issue of the stock-orders by the railroad, as already detailed. In January and February, 1840, state of Maryland bonds were sold by Baring Bros. & Co. at 85, the proceeds netting

$21,583.68 in Baltimore. This amount was applied by the railroad company to the payment of interest which had accrued, July 1, 1840, upon those bonds that had previously been sold in small lots.

During the summer and fall of 1839 a corps of engineers was engaged in surveying and laying out the line of the railroad from Harper's Ferry to Cumberland, so as to have it ready for the contractors to begin their operations in the spring of 1840. Another company of engineers began to survey a route for the railroad about the same time from Wheeling towards Cumberland, but the difficulties connected with making available the subscriptions to the railroad caused the abandonment of this part of the enterprise for the time. Nevertheless, although it was necessary for the railroad company to spend money continually in making extensive repairs, as well as to purchase and put upon the road new locomotives and cars, and although there were great financial difficulties, the work of extending the railroad from Harper's Ferry to Cumberland went steadily on after the spring of 1840.

Dividends of 2 and 3¼ per cent were declared in the fall of 1840 and 1841 respectively, but no dividend was declared in the fall of 1842, owing to the fact that all available means were being employed in completing the railroad to Cumberland, as well as because the city of Baltimore was unable to continue payments of instalments on its subscriptions. Over $2,465,000 had already been expended in continuing the railroad from Harper's Ferry, and this would practically have been lost had the railroad not been extended to Cumberland, or at least to Hancock, some fifty miles below Cumberland. At this crisis, therefore, the whole revenue of the railroad was applied in aid of the city subscription, after having deducted from this revenue the amounts needed for operating expenses, repair of the old road, etc., etc.

With the funds thus obtained the railroad was completed to a point opposite Hancock, 123 miles from Baltimore, on June 1, 1842, and five months later it was opened to Cumberland, 178 miles from Baltimore.

CHAPTER IV.

Embarrassment and Delay.

(1842-1848.)

It was not until the spring of 1849 that the actual extension of the railroad west of Cumberland was begun. The obstacles and embarrassments that caused this delay were many.

(1) By the laws of Maryland, Virginia and Pennsylvania, the railroad company had no authority without additional legislation to occupy any more territory for the construction of the road in any one of these states after 1843. The additional legislation desired was not obtained until after the expenditure of much time and trouble.

(2) The company lacked the money necessary to finish the railroad as planned, nor was the credit of the company good enough to raise the large sums needed.

(3) Such money as the railroad company did possess was urgently needed for the reconstruction of the road between Baltimore and Harper's Ferry and for new rolling stock.

These three classes of difficulties which prevented the extension of the road will be considered more in detail.

Delays in Legislation.

The charters of the railroad as granted by the states of Maryland and Virginia in 1827 provided that the road must be finished within these states within ten years from the time of the commencement of the railroad, otherwise the charters would be null and void. A similar provision was inserted in the act passed by Pennsylvania in February, 1828, authorizing the construction of a railroad by the Baltimore and Ohio Railroad Company through that state, except that "fifteen years" took the place of the words "ten years" in the Maryland and Virginia acts. On March 28, 1836,[1] an act was passed in the Maryland General Assembly extending the time for the completion of the railroad in Maryland to July 4, 1843. Such an act was necessary, for the road was then built only as far as a point opposite Harper's Ferry.

Even at that time the legislature of Virginia was dilatory in its action as regarded the railroad, and although the right to build in Virginia expired July 4, 1838, and the company, anxious to push the construction of the road on towards Cumberland, was doing everything in its power to secure the passage of a favorable bill in the Virginia legislature, it was not until April 2, 1838, that a law was passed extending the time allowed "for the completion of that portion of their improvement to be constructed within this commonwealth" to July 4, 1843. The other provisions of this act, upon the acceptance of which depended the extension of time, have already been treated.

But by November, 1842, the railroad had been constructed and opened only as far as Cumberland, a distance of but 178 miles. There were still two hundred miles of railroad to be built in order to unite Baltimore with "the waters of the West." A few months more and the company would have no rights of further extension in Maryland, Virginia or Pennsylvania, and by the terms of the charters conferred by these respective states the charters themselves were null and void if the railroad had not been completed within these states within the time specified.

For this last reason, even if it was impracticable to continue immediately the construction westward, it was necessary to secure a further extension of time in Maryland and in Virginia or Pennsylvania. A grant of such extension was obtained without difficulty from the Maryland legislature in 1843[2] in an act of much importance, since it not only extended the time for the completion of the railroad

---

[1] Acts of 1835, ch. 245.

[2] Maryland Laws, 1842, ch. 301.

in Maryland until July 5, 1863, but also provided for the sale of the state's interest in internal improvement companies and the payment of the state debts. But in spite of continued applications to the legislatures of Virginia and Pennsylvania, no acts at all acceptable to the company were forthcoming.

The Virginia legislature passed various acts granting the desired extension of time, but these laws contained so many vexatious restrictions regarding rates, taxation, routes, etc., that they were all rejected by the Baltimore and Ohio stockholders.

Finally, after a long and tedious period of application and petitioning, the Virginia legislature granted an act authorizing the extension of the railroad through Virginia on terms acceptable to the company. The act was passed March 6, 1847,[1] and accepted at a general meeting of the stockholders. This new law provided that the road was to be constructed to Wheeling according to the plans and route submitted by the chief engineer at a meeting of the stockholders held in Baltimore, July 12, 1845, with certain restrictions, however, that in order to secure to the city of Wheeling the benefit of the western terminus of the railroad, all parts thereof between the Monongahela river and Wheeling were to be opened for the transportation of passengers and freight simultaneously. The act also annulled the stock subscriptions on the part of the state of Virginia made by acts passed March 28, 1837, and April 2, 1838, which had provided for subscriptions of $302,100 and of $1,058,420 respectively. Provisions were also inserted reserving the right to connect with or intersect the railroad by other lines of transportation; obliging the company to erect certain depots, subjecting the company to the general railroad law of Virginia;[2] reserving the right of Virginia to tax the property, stock and profits of the company so far as these might be or

[1] Acts of Virginia Legislature, session 1846, ch. 99.

[2] Acts of Virginia Legislature, session 1837, ch. 118.

accrue in the commonwealth of Virginia on the same footing with other similar companies within the state; provided, however, that this taxing power was not to be exercised until and unless the net income of the railway company was over six per cent per annum upon the capital invested. The city of Wheeling was authorized to subscribe $1,000,000 to the capital stock of the railroad company upon such terms as might be agreed upon between the City Council of Wheeling and the company; and, again, that as a condition upon which the whole act was granted, the company was to "accept this act within six months and enter upon the construction of the continuation of their road hereinbefore authorized within three years, and complete the same within twelve years, after the passage of this act," *i. e.* by March 6, 1859.

So far as Maryland and Virginia were concerned, there were no further legal obstacles to the continuation of the railroad to the West. The charter had expired in Pennsylvania in 1843, and the act passed by the legislature of Pennsylvania, June 20, 1839, extending the time for the completion of the railroad in that state until February 27, 1847, was not accepted by the company, owing to the new and onerous conditions imposed by the act, especially those prescribing the route to be taken.

Financial Difficulties.

The years that were spent by the company in waiting for acceptable terms upon which to continue the extension of their railroad westward were not years wasted. At the time of the completion of the railroad to Cumberland the finances of the company were not in a condition to permit of new construction to any great extent or the expenditure of any large sums for such purposes. The money markets had not recovered in 1842 from the crisis and panic of 1837. As it was, the extension of the road to Cumberland from Harper's Ferry had only been made with much difficulty and skillful financiering. Although the railroad company had been able to realize from the $3,000,000 subscription of the city of Baltimore,[1] yet the credit of the state of Maryland was so low that its bonds had been a failure on the London market, and but £5,250 worth had been sold at 85. This sum had not been used in construction at all, but to pay interest on existing debts. The revenues of the railroad company and a loan by Baring Bros., with the state bonds as security, had together realized barely enough to enable the completion of the railroad to Cumberland.

The period between November, 1842, and the spring of 1849—when the active construction of the road toward Wheeling was finally begun—was spent in reconstructing those portions of the road east of Cumberland which were in need of improvement, in providing adequate rolling stock and preparing to make the financial arrangements requisite to ensure the completion of the road as soon as the necessary legislation regarding the right of way had been secured. It was evident to the directors at this time that the money necessary to completion could not be then obtained. The greater portion of the state bonds in payment of the $3,000,000 subscription still remained in the hands of the company, and indeed bade fair to so remain for an indefinite period.

In 1844 President McLane went to Europe for the second time in the interests of his company, to try to secure financial aid in the London market. He returned in October, 1846, without having accomplished his object, but his examination of the workings of the English railroads resulted in his submitting to the board of directors an improved method of organizing the operations of the road. The plan was adopted in 1847 and, with but a temporary suspension during the administration of President Swann (1848-1853), remained the permanent organization of the road for many years.[2]

---

[1] Session of 1836, Resolution No. 40. Approved March 17, 1836.

[2] The principal objects of the reform were to insure a proper adaptation and application of the supervisory power in each depart-

Almost immediately after the opening of the road to Cumberland it became necessary to reduce rates, owing to the fact that the Pennsylvania lines had met the prospective competition of the Baltimore and Ohio by lowering their rates considerably below those of their Maryland rival. Consequently charges for passengers on the Baltimore and Ohio were reduced about 25 per cent, and for freight about 30 per cent below the rates of the previous year. President McLane in his report[1] naïvely remarks that the Pennsylvania lines have established "rates which it is believed are not required by the public nor justified by the true interests of the works." Another disappointment to those interested in the Baltimore and Ohio was the fact that the wagon trans-

---

ment to the object under its immediate charge by means of a judicious division of labor; to effect a strict responsibility in the collection and disbursements of money, and in the accounting department generally by the multiplication of checks; to confine the company's mechanical operations in the shops to the purposes of repairs rather than of construction; and to promote the economical purchase and application of materials and the objects needed in every class of service. It was believed that all these ends could be best reached by confiding the departments of transportation, of the reconstruction and repairs of the road and of the repairs of machinery to separate superintendents of "Transportation," of "Road" and of "Machinery" respectively. Each of these departments was to be subject to the immediate supervision of a professional engineer under the general direction of the president of the road. All of these officers and all of the principal agents of the road were to be subject to annual appointment, and satisfactory security was to be required from each for faithful performance of duty.

Measures were also taken that the receipt of money be confined to as few agents as possible; for prompt payment from all of moneys received by them; for a new and securely guarded system of tickets to supersede the old, loose method by which counterfeiting was invited; for the imposition of further checks upon conductors and other agents, which were thought would prove more effective in enforcing a rigid accountability from all. A daily account was required of all agents with the secretary and treasurer of the railroad under the immediate supervision of the president in the central office of the company. It was evident too that the expense of the new system would be less, and that the efficiency would be much greater, than under the older and laxer system of general superintendents.

[1] Seventeenth Annual Report, p. 4.

portation over the National Road from the West failed to supply the anticipated traffic at Cumberland. This drawback was not fully obviated until the extension of the road to Wheeling in 1853. Still the completion of the railroad to such an important point as Cumberland showed immediate results in the augmentation of traffic, bearing out the claims of the presidents and directors that the more nearly the road was completed the larger, proportionally, would the net receipts become. Thus, for example, the receipts from passengers, mails and freight, the expenses for the same, and the net receipts for the four years 1841-44—the two years before and the two years after the road was finished to Cumberland—were as follows:

	RECEIPTS.			EXPENSES.	
Years.	Passengers and Mails.	Freight.	Total Receipts.		Net Receipts.
1841	$179,616	$211,454	$391,070	$239,622	$151,448
1842	181,177	245,315	426,492	216,715	209,777
1843	274,617	300,618	575,235	295,833	279,402
1844	336,876	321,743	658,619	311,633	346,986

The receipts from freight increased very rapidly after 1845.

Some such statement of the principles governing the earnings of but partially completed railroads was necessary to satisfy the demands of individuals who had their capital invested in Baltimore and Ohio stock, and who had seen very little return therefor, as well as to keep all alive to the absolute necessity of completion of the road to Wheeling, in order to realize the long hoped-for benefits that were expected to accrue from the great railroad. Although it was only too evident that the railway tracks and roadway generally east of Harper's Ferry were in need of thorough repairs, and in places even of reconstruction, and that money was needed for new rolling stock to satisfy the demands made for the transportation of goods from the region around and to the west of Cumberland, yet it was deemed expedient in the fall of 1843 to declare a dividend of 2 per cent upon the stock of the main line of the railroad. The dividend amounted to $140,000, or 2 per cent on $7,000,000. This amount of capital. however. was not all that upon which the dividend ought to have been declared, for surplus net revenue had been reinvested, *i. e.* used as capital, from 1830 onward, and by the fall of 1843 this sum amounted to $873,-806.

In the president's report[1] in which the above facts were announced, and indeed in all the reports from this time on and up to 1852, stress is laid upon the necessity of the completion of the work as orginially contemplated, the point being made that not only would the capital invested in an uncompleted line of railroad pay no dividends, but that the commerce and prosperity of Baltimore would be irretrievably injured by lack of communication with the West.

Need of Reconstruction and New Equipment.

The history of the railroad during this period is a story—so far as the practical workings and internal policy are concerned—of a struggle to survive and to remedy the serious mistakes made in the earlier years of the company's existence. The errors which cost the company so dear in the forties were mainly mistaken economies in construction and inadequate calculations as to the cost of a great and permanent railroad through an unfavorable territory. Ignorance in regard to railroad construction was at that time practically universal in America, and there was no school save that of experience in which the directors of the early railways could learn. In so far the early errors of the Baltimore and Ohio Railroad Company were unavoidable, but the experience was dearly bought.

Early in 1846 it became absolutely necessary to reconstruct entirely the line of road from Baltimore to Harper's Ferry, a distance of 81 miles, for the road as originally built was entirely inadequate for the heavy traffic for which

[1] Seventeenth Annual Report (1843).

it was being used. It was necessary, too, that the new "edge" rail be laid in place of the already antiquated "plate" rail. In January, 1846, the board of directors provided that thirty miles of road be immediately equipped with the new rails. The cost of this reconstruction was estimated at $316,800. The company had not the necessary funds at hand to pay for this except by taking the revenues of the road. It was possible to sell mortgage bonds on the open market only at a discount of at least ten per cent. Reasons for this were the low credit of the company, owing to its small dividends (never yet above 3 per cent), the absence of limit to the amount of bonds the company might issue and of proper provision for repayment. It was therefore resolved by the directors that the interests of the company and of the stockholders could be best served by applying net revenue to the amount of $1,000,000 to the further reconstruction of the railroad, and by issuing dividends to the stockholders up to the same amount, partly in the company's 6 per cent (second mortgage) bonds at par and partly in cash. The 3 per cent dividend declared September 30, 1846, was provided for as follows: "To all stockholders owning on the first day of October, 1846, less than 50 shares of stock, three dollars in money on each share on and after November 20, 1846; and to all similar stockholders owning 50 shares and over, one dollar on each share in money and two dollars in the bonds of the company, bearing 6 per cent interest, payable quarterly and reimbursable in twenty years." It was hoped that by these means the value of the company's bonds would be raised.

It was announced in the report of the president of the road for 1846 that owing to the state of the road necessitating not only reconstruction, but also a large future outlay on engines and cars (needed not only to replace those worn out, but also to purchase additional ones to accommodate the increasing traffic), no dividends were to be expected at the end of 1847, and that for the same reason "the dividend for the year ending September 30, 1848, will also be materially diminished." No further cash dividend was declared until May, 1856—a dividend of 3 per cent in bonds of the company being declared in 1847, and yearly dividends in additional stock of the company, *i. e.* "scrip," from 1848 to 1853 inclusive.

The work of reconstruction of the road was continued through 1847. Nearly $50,000 of the company's 6 per cent second mortgage bonds had been sold at about par, and the city of Baltimore had agreed to take $105,000 of the same securities at par as dividend. As regarded payments for the thirty miles of reconstruction authorized the previous year, the company had arranged to make part payment in the company's notes at long credit and part in the above-mentioned 6 per cent bonds at par. Furthermore, contracts had been made to the amount of $152,872 for alterations and improvements in the old track, and these contracts were to be payable also in the 6 per cent bonds at par. And finally, yet more of these 6 per cent bonds were used at par to pay the dividend of 3 per cent which was declared September 30, 1847.

The year 1848 was well spent in perfecting the workings of the railroad, in fostering economies by improvements in organization, construction and equipment, and in general preparation for the early extension of the road westward by careful reconnoissances and surveys of the region between Cumberland and Wheeling over the routes already fairly well known to the engineers. The next year witnessed the beginning of a period of renewed life, which did not end until the railroad had reached its western terminus at Wheeling.

When, in 1848, the company initiated its system of applying net revenue as capital in reconstructing and improvement and issuing stock dividends in lieu of money, it used part of this new capital in the purchase of ten first-class engines, two second-class engines, a third-class engine, 28 passenger cars and 171 freight cars. A branch of the railroad was extended to the south side of the harbor in Baltimore, where grounds were purchased at Locust Point. This was done so that freight not intended for distribution in the city might be carried by steam to the water's edge, and the expense and inconvenience of using horse-power through the streets of Baltimore avoided. Some $200,000 were also spent in general repairs of the road east of Harper's Ferry, and in straightening and changing the defective location of the track east of the Monocacy river, so that there might be no curve of less than 600 feet radius.

CHAPTER V.

COMPLETION. CUMBERLAND TO WHEELING.

(1848-1853.)

The administration of Thomas Swann, third president of the Baltimore and Ohio Railroad Company, covers the completion of the main stem, at that time the longest railroad in America. The construction in four years (1849-1852) of two hundred miles of railroad through the mountainous region of the Alleghanies, over ravines and rivers, through tunnels drilled in the rocky mountain-side, up steep ascents and around perilous curves, and above all, in face of a lack of the funds necessary to carry out fully the matured plans of the project, was an achievement only to be accomplished by a man of indefatigable energy, courage and indomitable will—a man at once a financier, an administrator and one possessing rare executive ability.

When Thomas Swann was elected president of the company shortly after McLane's resignation in 1848, his views on the expediency and necessity of speedy completion of the railroad to Wheeling were well known. He had already served the company as director and member of special committees appointed to secure favorable legislation for the railroad from the General Assembly of Virginia.

At a meeting of the board of directors held early in 1849, President Swann emphasized the fact that the friends of the railroad were becoming disheartened and many of the stockholders and the public generally were growing suspicious and unfriendly to the project, owing to the delays in its completion and inadequate returns upon their investments. The subscriptions of the state and city had caused an increase in taxation without any corresponding compensation. To put the railroad upon a paying basis, to ensure to Baltimore the commerce to which by virtue of geographical situation and natural advantages she was entitled, and finally to revive some of the old enthusiasm in the friends of the company, President Swann urged that active measures be at once taken to complete the railroad not only to Fairmont on the Monongahela river (as proposed by some of the directors), but to Wheeling on the Ohio river, as had been the original intention of the organizers of the company. President Swann did not overlook the difficulties, financial and topographical, which opposed the successful completion of this plan, but showed that the sacrifices already made in building the line of road then finished were much greater than those still to be made. His address is said to have had such an effect upon his hearers that George Brown, one of the directors and with Philip E. Thomas, co-founder of the company, is reported to have risen in excitement and moved "that the chief engineer be directed to arrange to put the whole line to the Ohio river under contract as speedily as practicable." The resolution was adopted with enthusiastic unanimity.

Reconnoissance of the country lying between Cumberland and Wheeling had been made as early as 1836 under direction of Benjamin H. Latrobe, and in his report he estimated the cost of building a railroad from Harper's Ferry to Wheeling, through Pittsburgh, at $9,500,000. In 1843 preliminary reconnoissances were made in the state of Virginia of the region lying between Cumberland and Wheeling. In July, 1847, Latrobe directed the operations of three corps of engineers engaged in the location of the proposed line of railway from Cumberland westward to the Maryland-Virginia boundary line. The party of engineers having the westernmost section in hand—but fifteen miles—on the completion thereof passed into Virginia, and by the close of the season some sixty miles of the route westward from Cumberland were ready for contract. In the summer and fall of 1848, Engineer Latrobe, induced by the difficulties of a suitable route over the mountains and across the valleys of the Cheat River and Tygart's Valley River regions, secured the services of two other expert engineers, who examined the entire region with care. The three engineers finally decided upon the routes that it would be best to follow, and reported also that in their opinion the construction of a railroad across this mountainous country was quite practicable with grades within the power of the locomotive.

All conditions at this time would have been favorable for the active extension of the road westward but for the lack of money. According to the estimate submitted by the general superintendent in October, 1849, the cost of the road from Cumberland to Wheeling was estimated at $6,278,000.

President Swann in his report for 1850 made the following exhibit of how much of this amount was to be raised, and how much of it the company then had or had already expended:

(1) Money expended for all purposes in the extension of the road west of Cumberland (Sept. 30, 1850), exclusive of bonds given for iron rails and interest	$ 934,713.56
(2) Balance of cash from sale of £200,000 5 per cent bonds	476,650.00
(3) Value of 5 per cent sterling bonds unsold (£507,500)	2,172,908.06[1]
(4) Bonds issued for iron rails (Jan. 1, 1850) at 6 per cent, for £127,500 secured by mortgage. Baring Brothers	566,666.67
(5) Revenue during progress of work, estimated at...	500,000.00
(6) Subscription of city of Wheeling	500,000.00
	$5,150,938.29
(7) Deficiency to be made up to enable the whole road to be placed under contract. Proposed to be raised by 6 per cent coupon bonds of the company	1,128,731.00
	$6,279,669.29
Estimated cost of the road (Cumberland to Wheeling) as per report of the general superintendent, Oct. 29, 1849	$6,278,000.00
[Actual cost	$6,631,721.00]

[1] The actual yield of these bonds was only $1,973,688.89, on account of their having been sold at a limit of 91 on January 3, 1851. Cf. Report of President for 1851, p. 8.

Taking into account the previous financial history of the railroad, the statement made a fairly satisfactory showing. Still it was not at all certain that the arrangements there shown could be actually carried out. Two of the items had already been financiered through by President Swann. The first deal was in regard to the Maryland state bonds issued in payment of the state's $3,000,000 subscription to the Baltimore and Ohio, and up to this time practically unsalable. These bonds were lying intact—with the exception of £5,000 sold in small lots—in the vaults of Baring Bros. of London as security for advances that that firm had made to the railroad company, and as a matter of policy, in that the opportunity for selling them would be better in London hands than in American. President Swann turned to these bonds as a means of raising revenue. They could be sold only if the credit of the state and of the railroad company[1] were raised by the active support of some such powerful London banking house as Baring Brothers. This support was secured after a long correspondence, and the London firm bought £200,000 of the 5 per cent sterling bonds of the state at a rate equal to that prevailing in the home market for the limited amount of these bonds offered for sale. It was hoped that the effect of this sale would be twofold—a reduction in the estimates of the probable cost of the road, owing to the confidence inspired by a full treasury; and a higher market rate for the remaining sterling bonds, due to the purchase made by such a conservative and powerful financial house as Baring Brothers. Both results did follow for a time, but other difficulties soon more than offset the advantages thus derived.[2]

---

[1] Shares of Baltimore and Ohio stock were sold in Baltimore in October, 1848, at 28.

[2] These bonds had been sold in limited amounts below par, but in his report for 1850 (p. 15) President Swann says that these bonds with the endorsement of Baring Bros. had sold in the London market during 1850 at from 105 to 108. The absolute necessity for money to finish the road led to a forced sale of the remaining bonds to a New York firm in January, 1851, at 91, realizing $1,973,688.89.

The second deal had for its object the raising of $566,-666.67 for the purchase of iron rails, and was also consummated through Baring Brothers. The railroad company issued £127,500 of 6 per cent mortgage bonds to Baring Brothers, payable in equal instalments in January, 1856, 1857, 1858, 1859 and 1860, and received in return some 20,000 tons of iron rails from Thompson & Foreman of London. These bonds were known as the "Iron Bonds."

The deficiency of $1,128,731, the sum needed to construct the railroad according to the estimate of October, 1849, was made up by the issuance to President Swann of 6 per cent mortgage bonds to the amount needed. The bonds were dated July 10, 1850, and were payable July 1, 1875. It was deemed inadvisable to put these bonds immediately upon the market, and they were not sold until 1852, when an unexpected crisis confronted the directors. The expenses of construction were then very large, the monthly average during the previous fiscal year having been $200,000. Five thousand laborers and over a thousand horses were then being employed by the company in the construction of new road. The treasury was growing alarmingly weak and it was found that the coupon bonds could not be floated at anything like par. The railroad must be completed at the earliest possible moment. Repeated efforts were therefore made to sell the bonds at a figure favorable to both the credit and the interests of the company, but were for a long time fruitless. The bonds were finally sold at a limit of 80, the directors feeling that it was better to make this comparatively small sacrifice for the time being rather than to endanger the existence of large and varied interests by indefinite delay in the completion of the work.

Legislation regarding the railroad during the period from 1849 to 1853 was comparatively unimportant, except for an act passed March 21, 1850, by the legislature of Virginia. The reasons for the passage of this act were as follows: By the law passed by the Virginia legislature, March 6, 1847 (Ch. 99, Acts of 1846-7), it had been provided that extension of time for completion through Virginia depended among other things upon the railroad being made to enter the ravine of the Ohio river not south of the mouth of Fish Creek in Marshall County, with the further provision "that if the said railroad by the cheapest route to the city of Wheeling, which shall not enter the ravine of the Ohio river at any point south of Grave Creek in Marshall County, shall appear from the estimates to be made as aforesaid to be *more* costly to construct, maintain and work than it would be by the route passing into the ravine of the Ohio river at or near the mouth of Fish Creek and thence to the city of Wheeling; and if, when the difference of probable cost between said two routes shall be ascertained as aforesaid, the city of Wheeling shall agree to pay to said railroad such difference of cost by the time said railroad shall be completed and opened for transportation to said depot in Wheeling (which payment it shall be lawful for the said city of Wheeling to provide for and make), then the said railroad company are hereby required to locate and construct their said railroad so that in passing to said depot in Wheeling it shall not enter the ravine of the Ohio river at any point south of Grave Creek."

Since the time of the completion of the Baltimore and Ohio to Cumberland it had been the desire of the company to build its road in as straight and southerly a line to the Ohio as possible, in order to connect with Cincinnati and St. Louis over the shortest line of road, and it was not at all desirous of making Wheeling the terminus of the main stem. The people of Wheeling, on the other hand, fearing with much reason that the more southerly the line of the Baltimore and Ohio the greater danger of their commerce and industry being unfavorably affected, owing to the short and direct connection of Baltimore and the Atlantic seaboard with Cincinnati and St. Louis, had made every effort to make the railroad take the most northerly route to their city. The citizens of Wheeling therefore decided upon the Grave Creek or more northerly route; the directors of the

Baltimore and Ohio, looking to what they considered their own best interests, decided upon the Fish Creek route. As a matter of course, controversy and dissension followed. As a consequence, the citizens of Wheeling proposed to make an application to the Virginia legislature to stop the progress of the railroad in that state. President Swann went to the legislature and succeeded in counteracting this application, but a law was passed, March 21, 1850, providing for a board of three engineers, "not residents of the states of Maryland, Virginia, Pennsylvania or Ohio, and not interested in or in any manner connected with the said company or the said city," which board was to render a final and binding decision after full investigation of the matter in dispute. From a desire to avoid further delay in the completion of the road, since the above-mentioned board of engineers had made a decision[1] adverse to the company, President Swann advised the Baltimore and Ohio stockholders, at a general meeting held in May, 1850, to give way to the desires of the people of Wheeling and build along the Grave Creek route. This was accordingly done, and what had bidden fair to be a long and stubbornly contested controversy was thus averted by the conciliatory policy of the railroad.

The city of Wheeling, by the agreement of 1847 with the railroad company, had stipulated to furnish free of charge, with the right of way through the city streets, a depot on the north side of Wheeling Creek with not less than two acres of ground. By a compromise between the city and the company the agreement of 1847 was abrogated and another made, whereby Wheeling agreed to pay $50,000 of the $78,000 estimated as the cost of the Wheeling depot. The railroad company agreed to do this because the latter sum included in its purchasing power a considerable plot of ground that would not be needed by the railroad and that, it was believed, could be sold for more than the $28,000 difference.

---

[1] Cf. Report, 1850, p. 13.

It was felt that for the next few years the railway would have to depend upon the navigation of the Ohio river to a considerable extent as regarded communication with Cincinnati, St. Louis and other points beyond the western terminus of the road. But a passenger ascending the Ohio river in a steamboat could reach Baltimore in about the same time it would take him to reach Pittsburgh, since Wheeling was a day's journey by boat from Pittsburgh. The importance of a line of boats connecting with the Baltimore and Ohio schedule was clearly seen, and a company was organized in 1852 under a charter passed by the Virginia legislature, whereby a daily line of boats "of a class superior to any yet floated upon the Western waters," was to be ready to run on the Ohio by January 1, 1853, in connection with the Baltimore and Ohio to Cincinnati and Louisville.

With affairs in such a condition as regarded the future, although the company had a large bonded debt and the need of a second track and an ampler equipment soon became evident, it was no wonder that the spirits of those who had worked hard in bringing the enterprise to a successful completion were elevated and that they looked with confidence and assurance to the years to come.

While the new road from Cumberland to Wheeling was in process of construction it was the policy of the company to keep the line east of Cumberland in the very best possible condition, having by this time learned that the most expensively built railroad is really the cheapest, and that immediate and careful attention to minor repairs effects great economies. Simple and evident as this appears, it had by no means always been acted upon. Preparations were also being made to increase the capacity of the road from its limited power in 1848, so as better to meet the traffic which it was confidently felt the completion of the main stem would develop. The means by which this was done were by issuing dividends in the form of additional stock and using the net receipts, which the stock dividends represented, as additional capital applied to construction. The following "scrip" or stock dividends were thus declared: 3½ per cent, payable in November, 1848; 5 per cent, payable in November, 1849; 7 per cent, payable in November, 1850; 7 per cent, payable in November, 1851; 7 per cent, payable in November, 1852; and 3 per cent, payable in May, 1853.

During this period of completion of the railroad to Wheeling the company made many other provisions for perfecting their road. New engines and cars were ordered, so that in January, 1853, the company had 139 engines, 96 passenger cars and 2567 freight cars. In 1852 the ground was bought upon which Camden Station, the present principal depot of the Baltimore and Ohio in Baltimore, now stands, and preparations were made to erect a suitable building and train-shed. Permission was given to the company by the city to approach the new depot by steam locomotive, thereby obviating the expense of horse-power. The Mt. Clare shops, at which 1,000 men were employed during 1852, had also been much enlarged during this period, and many improvements had been made upon the company's property at Cumberland and Martinsburg. The facilities afforded by the railroad for the cheap transportation of coal to tide-water had led to the opening and development of many mines in and around the Cumberland and Frostburg regions. The large increase in the coal trade led to the need of enlarged facilities for handling coal at Baltimore, and new wharves, fitted completely for transferring thousands of tons of coal to waiting vessels, were erected at Locust Point, not only by the railroad company, but also on private account.

The building of the new road westward proceeded rapidly and uninterruptedly in spite of financial and topographical obstacles. In the twenty-third annual report of the Baltimore and Ohio in October, 1849, President Swann was able to announce that 103½ miles had been put under contract, and those at very advantageous prices. During the next official year ending September 30, 1850, the work was pressed on. The action of the board of engineers appointed under the act of March 21, 1850, by the legislature of Virginia had led the stockholders and directors of the company to decide to use the Grave Creek route, and work was accordingly being done upon it. In spite of the fact that there had been a scarcity of labor during the previous year, 167 miles of road were announced as under way. Some 3,500 laborers and 700 horses were engaged on this work during 1850. The rails were laid during the spring of 1851, and in July of that year the road was formally opened to Piedmont, twenty-eight miles west of Cumberland.

Not quite a year after the opening to Piedmont (June 22, 1852) the road was opened to Fairmont on the Monongahela river, 124 miles from Cumberland and but 77 miles from Wheeling. The location of this road through one of the boldest mountain regions which had yet been traversed by any work of internal improvement in America is said to have excited surprise even among professional engineers. For more than seventy miles the road had been built across a succession of mountain ranges. The Monongahela river was crossed by a viaduct 650 feet long and 39 feet above low water, the iron superstructure supported by the massive abutments forming what was then the largest iron bridge in America. Between Cumberland and Wheeling eleven tunnels were bored, making together a total of 11,156 feet in length. The three largest were 4,100 feet, 2,350 feet and 1,250 feet in length respectively. Between the same points there were 113 bridges with a total length of 7,003 feet and ranging from 12 to 205 feet span.

On Christmas Eve, 1852, the last rail was laid and the last spike driven. Baltimore had finally been connected with the "western waters" by bonds of iron. President Swann's hopes and predictions, in the face of innumerable and apparently insurmountable obstacles, were fulfilled. On the first of January, 1853, the first train to make the complete trip from Baltimore to Wheeling rolled through the streets of that city bearing the first of the five hundred guests who came to participate in the formal celebration of the completion of the Baltimore and Ohio Railroad.

CHAPTER VI.

General Results.

During the period of construction of the Baltimore and Ohio Railroad from Baltimore to Wheeling the enterprise exercised important influences upon the growth of the wealth and the development of the resources of Maryland. It is not easy to put into figures or to estimate the exact contribution of the railroad to the economic interests of the country along its route. But in a general way these effects can be indicated by statements regarding the part played by the railroad in the development of the towns and of the mineral, agricultural and other resources of the state. The development of the natural wealth of Maryland led to an increase in trade and commerce as well as in manufactures. This in turn exerted important influence upon the growth of the towns and, more especially, of Baltimore.

Had the Baltimore and Ohio Railroad not been built at the time and by the means actually employed, some other line of railroad would undoubtedly have been constructed sooner or later, connecting Baltimore with the West. Such a railroad if built at a later date might have been constructed at a smaller apparent cost, but it is doubtful if the real cost would have been less. For in 1827 a railroad to the West was a necessity brooking no delay, and although the Baltimore and Ohio up to the completion to Wheeling paid no adequate dividends to its stockholders, yet it paid largely to the people of Maryland in a positive way by developing their resources, and in a negative way by preventing the loss of the internal trade of Maryland and of the West.

Effects upon the Industries of Maryland.

The effect of the railroad in stimulating the industries of Maryland is perhaps nowhere better shown than in the development of coal mines, iron mines and quarries.

Before the railroad reached Cumberland in November, 1842, the rich coal deposits of Western Maryland had been practically unworked. The residents of Frostburg, then a straggling hamlet, and some of the residents of Cumberland had been in the habit of digging a few hundreds of bushels out of the surface veins during the winter. This coal was loaded on flat-boats and floated down to Alexandria by means of the spring floods which deepened the Potomac. Here boats and cargo were sold and the crews generally walked back to Cumberland.

With the extension of the railroad to Cumberland real work in the mines began. Several contracts were made between the railroad and mining companies for the transportation of coal and iron to the eastern market, and the railroad company commenced to provide better facilities in the way of cars, side-tracks and switches for the rapid carriage of mineral freights. Large coal wharves were built by the railroad company at Locust Point in Baltimore to provide easy means of transhipment of coal from the cars to the holds of vessels, and the building of similar private wharves was encouraged by the offer of a lower rate for the transportation of coal. By 1850 the rich coal region around Cumberland and Frostburg had already been much developed, and the demand for this coal was increasing more rapidly than the facilities needed to bring it to market. In 1851 several companies owning lands in the coal basin about Westernport began to open mines along the line of road west of Cumberland. The traffic received a temporary check in the winter of 1852, owing to the failure of the Maryland Mining Company in October, 1851, and the heavy rates of pilotage of vessels entering and leaving the harbor of Baltimore during the opening months of 1852, but the business soon began to increase beyond its former volume, and by the fall of 1852 the company had applications for coal contracts aggregating several thousand tons per day. Much coal freight was also expected from the piercing of a vast coal basin by the George's Creek Railway, under construction in 1852 and planned to connect with the Baltimore and Ohio at Piedmont. Before 1843 there is no mention of the transportation of any coal whatever over the Baltimore and Ohio. During that year but 4,964 tons were transported. In 1850 the shipments of coal eastward over the Baltimore and Ohio aggregated 132,534 tons; in 1851, 139,110 tons, and in 1852, in spite of many obstacles to the traffic, 132,306 tons.

The iron deposits of the state, although worked earlier, were not developed to such an extent as the coal mines. 1,574 tons of iron were shipped to the east in 1832; five years later the year's shipment amounted to 4,883 tons. The amount of iron began to decrease after this until the road reached Cumberland, when the working of the iron deposits in Alleghany county led to largely increased shipments, not only of iron, but also of iron ore. In 1851, 10,956 tons of iron and 4,386 tons of iron ore were shipped to the east.

The extension of the Baltimore and Ohio likewise greatly encouraged the opening of quarries. The shipment of granite, lime, soapstone and limestone to the east amounted in some years to over 10,000 tons, whereas the high cost of transportation had heretofore made the working of quarries, except in the immediate vicinities of the large towns, unprofitable. Fire-brick was shipped during and after 1849 at the rate of hundreds of tons per year.

Flour and tobacco were the principal agricultural products of Maryland during this period, and the extension of the railroad westward is marked by an increasing shipment of these commodities to the eastern market. Before the construction of the railroad these products had been brought by wagons to Baltimore, but at considerable expense and with many delays incident to unfavorable weather. Ellicott's Mills was a center of the flouring industry, and the construction of the railroad to this particular place was caused by the need of adequate facilities for the transportation of flour from the mills to tide-water in Baltimore.

In the year ending September 30, 1832, some 12,610 tons

of flour (146,936 barrels) were carried by the railroad from Ellicott's Mills and Frederick to Baltimore. In 1842 twice as many tons (25,233) were shipped eastwardly through the state via the Baltimore and Ohio, and in 1852 no less than 66,377 tons were so shipped. The encouragement given to agriculture is also shown by the fact that but 353 tons of grain were shipped eastward in 1832, while in 1852 nearly 5000 tons were so shipped.

The shipments of tobacco increased from 174 tons in 1832 to 1,510 tons in 1843, and to 2,322 tons in 1848, but diminished in size in the next few years. Shipments of meal increased from 512 tons in 1832 to 3,174 tons in 1852.

Maryland was not noteworthy as a cattle-raising state, and the live stock needed in Baltimore for local consumption was driven to town from the nearby regions along the highways. But with the westward extension of the railroad a slowly increasing demand arose for cattle from the interior. There is no record at all of live-stock shipped eastward in 1832; in 1834 only 23 tons were so shipped. In 1843, a year after the railroad had been completed to Cumberland, 1,219 tons of live-stock were transported to the east, and in 1849 the maximum of 18,991 tons was reached.

After the railroad reached Cumberland lard and butter acquired some prominence as articles of eastern shipment, amounting in some years to nearly 1,800 tons.

Whiskey was an important article of shipment, the amount shipped east increasing from 66 tons in 1832 to 1,111 tons in 1848. Bark for tanning purposes, leather and firewood were other commodities which were given a new value in the places of their production through the facility and cheapness of transportation afforded by the railroad. General farm products, such as potatoes, cabbage, vegetables, fruits, etc., also found a wider and better market with the operation of the railroad. After the railroad reached Cumberland the shipments of these products increased from hundreds to thousands of tons.

Growth of Towns.

The opening of the road marked the beginning of a new era in the history of Cumberland. The city was made the point of exchange for passengers and merchandise between East and West. Hotels and warehouses were erected. The facilities afforded for rapid transportation over the mountains greatly increased the travel between Cumberland and the West. This is evidenced by the larger use of the National Road after the completion of the railroad to Cumberland. From March 1 to March 20, 1849, no less than 2,586 passengers were carried over the National Road. In 1830 the population of Cumberland was 1,162, in 1840 it was 2,384, and in 1850 in was 6,105. When the Baltimore and Ohio was completed to Wheeling in 1853 the effect was soon felt in Cumberland. Most of the stage lines were taken off and the business of transferring merchandise was greatly diminished. But Cumberland continued to grow in wealth and population, and in this growth the railroad played an important part.[1]

The effect of the extension of the railroad upon the development of other Maryland towns was almost immediately beneficial, although not always capable of accurate measurement. When Frederick was connected with Baltimore in December, 1831, a ready market for the products of the surrounding region was established and land values were enhanced. The effect upon reaching Point of Rocks has been described.[2] The completion to Harper's Ferry secured connection with the Potomac and Winchester Railroad, penetrating the most fertile parts of Virginia. Harper's Ferry marking both a physical and commercial break in transportation, grew in population, wealth and importance after this time.

Before the railroad reached Cumberland, Frostburg was but a straggling village of a few hundred souls.[3] After the

---

[1] Cf. W. H. Lowdermilk, "History of Cumberland," pp. 349-376.

[2] See above, pp. 26–27.

J. T. Scharf, "History of Western Maryland," Vol. II.

opening of the mines, due to the railroad, a number of mining companies set actively to work, employing hundreds of men and establishing the nucleus of a flourishing and prosperous town.

The railroad was a great stimulus to the growth of the population, trade, manufactures and wealth of the city of Baltimore during the period from 1827 to 1853. Nearly 2,000,000 tons of commodities, including flour, tobacco, grain, live-stock, coal, iron, wood, leather and building stone, were shipped into Baltimore from the West alone via this railroad during this period, and either distributed by Baltimore shipping or utilized in new local manufactures. By the time the railroad was completed to Wheeling the industries of Baltimore included iron and copper works, woolen and cotton manufactures, flouring mills, manufacturers of white-lead, glass, shot, printer's ink, types, pottery, agricultural implements, powder, carpetings, house furniture, hats, cloth, etc., as well as distilleries and sugar refineries.[1] Not only had the railroad encouraged the establishment of these industries by transporting to Baltimore at low cost the raw materials required, but it also distributed in part the manufactured products throughout Maryland. Thousands of tons of these commodities were transported westward by the railroad every year, as well as large quantities of fish and oysters from the Chesapeake Bay, which were unloaded at the Baltimore wharves. During 1852 over 75,000 tons of merchandise were transported westwardly. The commodities shipped included salt, coffee, sugar, molasses, fish, oysters, lumber, plaster, dry-goods, manufactured iron, furniture, vehicles and machinery, drugs and paints, oils, groceries, guano and manures, bricks, etc. About 8,500 tons went to Frederick, 3,350 tons to Harper's Ferry, 9,500 to Winchester, 1,350 to Martinsburg, 24,500 to Cumberland, and nearly 30,000 tons to other points along the road.[2]

---

[1] De Bow, "Industrial Resources of the South and West," Vol. I, p. 103.

[2] Apropos of the dependence of Baltimore upon the West, J. H. B. Latrobe remarked at a banquet given in honor of the opening

Finances of the Railroad.

During the period from 1827 to 1853 the finances of the Baltimore and Ohio present none of those complexities which appeared in the later history of the railroad. The organization of the company and the management of its business were directed to the single object of making the road an efficient channel of communication between the East and the West. The company had no speculative purposes in view, but simply attempted to make the railroad a paying investment to the *bona fide* stockholders. This policy was consistently carried out. The company's stocks represented actual money paid in for the purpose of constructing and equipping the railroad. They were not watered for the profit of the originators of the road. Even when "scrip" was issued, from 1848 to 1853, it represented net earnings applied to construction and repairs, and was not issued simply to reduce nominal dividends.

The bonds issued by the railroad company during this period were for money urgently needed. Although some of these bonds were sold as low as 80 with par at 100, yet the sales seem to have been justified by the necessity of finishing the road. This alone could make the railroad pay any returns, or indeed prevent the practical loss of a large part of the sums already expended.

The dividends during the period 1827-1853 were as follows:

January, 1831	$0.37½
January, 1832	.60
July, 1832	.75
February, 1833	.75
October, 1835	1.12½

of the railroad to Wheeling in January, 1853, "The West built up Baltimore—first with the pack-saddle, then with the country road, then with the turnpike, and is now about to employ the greatest agent of modern times to realize the destiny appointed by Providence."

October, 1840		$2.00
October, 1841		2.00
October, 1843		2.00
October, 1844		2.50
October, 1846	($1 cash, $2 bonds)	3.00
November, 1847	($3 in bonds at 6%)	3.00
November, 1848	(stock)	3.50
November, 1849	(stock)	5.00
November, 1850	(stock)	7.00
November, 1851	(stock)	7.00
November, 1852	(stock)	7.00
May, 1853	(stock)	3.00

From the above enumeration it will be seen that the railroad at no time during this period was really a paying investment to the stockholders. The railroad paid only in the sense that it preserved and increased the trade of Baltimore with the West. The road was practically built three times east of Harper's Ferry during this period, and the great cost of construction, equipment and repairs prevented any large net earnings.

The issue of stock-orders by the company in 1839 and 1840, as detailed above,[1] was a financial measure which served the railroad well by enabling it to make use of Baltimore's subscription at a time when funds were needed and the possibility of floating the city stock doubtful. That the stock-orders circulated for a time at par and as currency, however, does not prove at all that such a form of money was desirable. The eventual depreciation of the certificates worked much hardship to laborers obliged to receive them in payment for work. Public opinion was roused to such an extent that in March, 1846, the legislature of Maryland prohibited the railroad company from issuing "anything in the nature of a bank note or other paper to be used for circulation as a currency."[2]

---

[1] See pages 47–48. [2] Acts of Maryland Assembly, 1845, ch. 313.

While the general financial policy of the company was to complete the road as originally projected as soon as possible, in order to secure for the stockholders adequate returns on their investments, yet the particular manner in which the policy was carried out differed somewhat under the three presidents of the railroad who guided its affairs during this period.

Under President Philip E. Thomas (1827-1836) the magnitude of the undertaking was not clearly seen, and consequently adequate provisions were not made for securing the capital necessary to carry the work to completion. A policy, perhaps too cautious, was pursued with regard to expenditures, and profits were divided which were too small to be advantageously distributed and which would have been more effective if used in the improvement and extension of the road.

During the administration of President Louis McLane (1836-1848) the results of this policy became evident. A cheaply constructed and imperfectly planned railroad proved not only entirely inadequate for the purposes for which it was needed, but its defects were the cause of the expenditure of large sums of money for repairs and reconstruction, which ought to have been available for the extension of the road to Cumberland. To add to the difficulties of the company came the panic of 1837. The years 1838 and 1839 were the darkest in the history of the Baltimore and Ohio during the whole period before 1853, and work had to be suspended. With the help of city and state loans the company resumed construction and net receipts began to increase. From 1836 to 1840 the company used its earnings for new construction, and borrowed only where absolutely necessary to keep the road in running order. The device of paying some dividend in order to raise the credit of the company was employed from 1840 to 1847.

The policy of President Thomas Swann (1848-1853) was the completion of the road to the Ohio at any cost as a condition precedent to its successful operation. Earnings were used as capital and dividends declared in stock; bonds were issued to be sold at a high price if possible; but, in any event, to be sold. Everything that would perfect the road with regard to the route and to equipment was tried. To obtain the carrying trade of Virginia, the Winchester and Potomac Railroad was bought. Acts of the Virginia legislature were accepted not altogether to the liking of the company in order to complete the railroad to Wheeling. It was confidently expected that adequate returns on capital would be secured after that point had been reached. The financial policy of President Swann may be summed up in the phrase, "Finish the railroad as rapidly and as thoroughly as possible; it will pay, no matter what it may seem to cost."

The Maryland legislature acted as a real arbitrator between the Baltimore and Ohio Railroad and the Chesapeake and Ohio Canal, not only in regard to right of way, but also in the attempt to arrange for a division of traffic on the two lines of transportation. An attempt of the Maryland legislature to secure the co-operation of the two companies in the transportation of coal from Cumberland is an instance in point.

The fixing of rates by Maryland and Virginia in the charters and in subsequent legislation has been previously noted. The railroad was regarded during the earlier part of this period as essentially a special kind of highway or toll road. The rates were generally fixed as maximum rates, and at first were based entirely on weight.[1]

The state of Maryland and the city of Baltimore occupied a unique position during most of this period by the exercise of direct control over the affairs of the railroad company. As stockholders they were entitled to have directors to represent their interests; but these directors were not elected

---

[1] Some of the laws fixing rates are: Maryland Acts, 1826, ch. 123, sec. 18; 1830, ch. 117; 1835, ch. 395, sec. 9; 1836, ch. 261; 1840, ch. 86; 1840, ch. 370. Virginia Acts: Charter, 1827; 1837, ch. 118, sec. 24; 1839, ch. 98, sec. 4, etc.

by the general body of stockholders, but were appointed by the governor in the case of the state, and by the joint ballot of both branches of the City Council in the case of the city. Baltimore was given two directors in the company for its first subscription of 5,000 shares in 1827, and one director for each 5,000 shares of its subsequent subscription of $3,000,000 in 1836. The city was to have in no case more than twelve directors in all. Maryland had two directors for the subscription of 5,000 shares in 1827 and was authorized to appoint one additional director for each 5,000 shares subscribed in 1835, on account of the $3,000,000 subscription. When the state sold its interest in the Baltimore and Ohio (authorized by act of Assembly of 1842, ch. 301, passed March 10, 1843) the right of appointing directorships of course stopped.

The beginnings of discrimination in rates between competitive and non-competitive points are to be noted in the early years of the company. Petitions were received from time to time after 1840 from merchants engaged in the flour trade in Baltimore, stating that in consequence of the low rates charged on the Chesapeake and Ohio Canal the shipments of flour were being rapidly diverted from the Baltimore market to the District of Columbia. The flour trade had always been considered of great importance to the prosperity of Baltimore, and as long as communication with the interior had been kept up by turnpikes almost the entire product of Maryland and of a considerable portion of Pennsylvania and Virginia had been brought to the Baltimore market and had constituted a most important element in the growth and prosperity of that city. But owing to the competition in transportation due to the above-mentioned canal and the Cumberland Valley Railroad—extending from Chambersburg to Philadelphia—the flour inspections at Baltimore for several years past, instead of having increased with the growth and settlement of the country, had scarcely equaled those of an earlier period. Reduction in rates of transportation was therefore asked for.

The board of directors of the railroad recognizing that not only the trade in flour would be further diverted from the Baltimore market, but also a considerable portion of business more or less inseparably connected with the flour trade, entailing not only a serious loss to the city, but also a definite and absolute loss of traffic to the railroad, resolved in 1845 to reduce charges *only along that portion of the road which was adjacent to the Chesapeake and Ohio Canal* to a minimum which would at least pay the expenses of transportation. This is perhaps one of the very earliest instances on record of discriminations in rates due to the rivalry of competitive points. Nothing was done to prohibit this at the time.[1]

Improvements in Technique.

The Baltimore and Ohio Railroad, as one of the pioneer roads in America, encountered and solved many difficult problems in the mechanics of railroading. Car wheels, for example, were first constructed with the flange on the inside edge. This caused many a derailment and many a broken wheel, and led to the invention of the outside flange car wheel. Still the wheel was unsatisfactory, especially in turning curves, and the invention of the conical flange was the result. Car wheels at this time were constructed of cast iron. To the Baltimore and Ohio must also be attributed the anti-friction box on the axles of the car wheels, and the use of the eight-wheeled car, both inventions of Ross Winans. During the period 1830 to 1853 radical and im-

[1] Virginia passed a law, March 6, 1847 (Acts of Virginia, 1846, ch. 99) against discrimination in rates on the Baltimore and Ohio Railroad with regard to long and short hauls, forbidding the company to "charge for transportation or travel to or from Baltimore from or to any point distant more than five miles in a direct line from the Ohio river more in the aggregate than for transportation or travel from Wheeling to Baltimore, or from Baltimore to Wheeling respectively, nor more in the aggregate from any depot west of Harper's Ferry to Baltimore, or from Baltimore to such depot, than from any other depot more distant from Baltimore to Baltimore, or from Baltimore to such last-mentioned depot."

portant changes were made in the construction of steam locomotives, and the introduction of the " Grasshopper " and " Camel " types are due to the Baltimore and Ohio and its engineers. When completed to Wheeling the road-bed embodied the results of the highest engineering skill in construction over the Alleghany mountains, and included the longest railroad bridges and trestles and the longest tunnels of any railroad in America. Many valuable improvements in track-construction, road-bed, stringers, ballast, switches, turn-outs, and especially in the method of laying of rails for turning sharp curves, are attributable to the Baltimore and Ohio Railroad.

---

[1] See " Address " by President Mendes Cohen, delivered before the American Society of Civil Engineers, June, 1892, " Proceedings," pp. 535-558.

VII.—APPENDIX

1.—Chronology of the Baltimore and Ohio Railroad.

First general meeting of citizens contemplating a railroad, February 12, 1827.
Act of incorporation granted by Maryland, February 28, 1827.
Act of incorporation confirmed by Virginia, March 8, 1827.
Requisite amount of stock for organization subscribed by April 1, 1827.
Company organized; directors elected, April 23, 1827.
Preliminary surveys begun, July 2, 1827.
Actual surveys begun, November 20, 1827.
Charter confirmed by the state of Pennsylvania, February 22, 1828.
Maryland became a stockholder, March 6, 1828.
Corner-stone laid, July 4, 1828.
Railroad opened to Ellicott's Mills, 14 miles (horse-power), May 22, 1830.
Trial of the first steam locomotive on the Baltimore and Ohio Railroad, August 25, 1830.
Railroad opened to—
  Ellicott's Mills, 14 miles (steam-power), August 30, 1830.
  Frederick, 61 miles, December 1, 1831.
  Point of Rocks, 69 miles, April 1, 1832.
  Harper's Ferry, 81 miles, December 1, 1834.
  Hancock, 123 miles, June 1, 1842.
  Cumberland, 178 miles, November 5, 1842.
  Piedmont, 206 miles, July 21, 1851.
  Fairmont, 302 miles, June 22, 1852.
Last spike driven; finished, Baltimore to Wheeling, 379 miles, December 24, 1852.
First train reached Wheeling from Baltimore, January 1, 1853.
Railroad opened, Baltimore to Wheeling, 379 miles, January 10, 1853.

2.—Cost of Construction.

Baltimore to Harper's Ferry	$ 4,000,000.00
Harper's Ferry to Cumberland	3,623,606.28
Cumberland to Wheeling	6,631,721.00
First cost of 379 miles of railroad	$14,255,327.28
Cost of reconstruction, etc., east of Cumberland	962,589.02
Extension to Locust Point	180,205.63
Camden Street Station (ground)	230,841.31
Grand total	$15,628,963.24

Estimated cost of construction (Feb., 1827), $5,000,000.

Real cost of construction (Jan., 1853), $15,628,963.24.

Estimated length of road (Balto. to the Ohio river) (Feb., 1827), 290 miles.

Real length of road (Balto. to the Ohio river) (Jan., 1853), 379 miles.

Estimated revenues per annum (Feb., 1827), $750,000.00.

Real revenues per annum (Oct. 1, 1853), $2,033,419.80.

3.—STATEMENT OF TRADE, REVENUE, PROFITS AND DIVIDENDS OF THE B. & O. R. R. FROM THE OPENING IN 1830 TO COMPLETION TO WHEELING, OCT. 1852.

Years ending October 1.	RECEIPTS.									EXPENSES.	NET RECEIPTS.	DIVIDENDS.		Surplus reinvested.
	PASSENGERS.				TONNAGE.			TOTAL RECEIPTS.						
	Carried in Washington Branch trains.	Carried in Main Stem trains.	Total number of passengers on both roads.	Receipts from passengers and mails.	East-ward freight. Tons.	West-ward freight Tons.	Total freight. Tons.	Passengers and tonnage.	Receipts from tonnage alone.	Total for passengers and tonnage.		Per cent.	Amount.	
1830	....	....	....	....	....	....	....	$ 14,711	....	$ 11,985	$ 2,726	.37½%		
1831	....	81,905	81,905	$ 27,250	3,876	2,055	5,931	31,405	$ 4,155	10,995	20,410	.60%	$69,975	$ 15,326
1832	....	89,022	89,022	67,910	29,445	11,640	41,085	136,937	69,027	75,673	61,264	.75%		
1833	....	88,633	88,633	83,233	37,166	25,589	62,755	195,680	112,447	138,495	57,195	.75%	30,061	27,134
1834	....	94,844	94,844	89,182	36,192	19,929	56,121	205,437	116,255	138,402	67,035	....	....	67,035
1835	12,147	85,611	97,758	93,540	46,979	25,655	72,634	263,368	169,828	161,216	102,152	1.12½%	45,002	57,150
1836	75,416	81,686	157,102	128,126	40,805	25,898	66,703	281,312	153,186	212,937	68,375	....	....	68,375
1837	73,474	67,225	140.699	145,625	40,697	33,901	74,598	301,301	155,676	289,125	12,176	..	....	12,116
1838	83,749	66,676	150,516	166,694	47,447	30,079	77,526	365,224	198,530	271,581	93,643	....	....	93,643
1839	86,964	65,537	152,501	173,860	54,573	45,878	100,451	407,347	233,487	312,700	94,647	....	....	94,647
1840	87,202	65,216	152,418	177,035	62,736	25,638	88,374	432,885	255,848	275,189	157,694	2%	80,000	77,694
1841	107,136	64,493	171,629	179,616	42,056	23,443	65,499	391,070	211,454	239,622	151,448	2%	130,000	21,448
1842	94,566	60,002	154,568	181,177	37,600	30,243	67,843	426,492	245,315	216,715	209,777	....	....	209,777
1843	78,425	71,108	149,533	274,617	55,523	27,191	82,714	575,235	300,618	295,833	279,402	2%	140,000	139,402
1844	99,106	74,661	173,821	336,876	69,886	33,224	103,110	658,619	321,743	311,633	346,986	2½%	175,000	171,986
1845	103,588	98,870	202,458	369.882	90,865	50,541	141,406	738,603	368,721	363,841	374,762	....	...	374,762
1846	157,157	123,107	280,264	413,341	110.356	83,559	193,915	881,687	468,346	454,840	426,747	3*a*	210,000	216,847
1847	151,753	136.921	288,674	447,020	183,824	79,511	263,335	1,101,937	654,917	590,829	511,108	3*b*	210,000	301,108
1848	170,196	160,974	331,170	488,376	205,174	66,078	271,252	1,213,664	725,288	662,106	551,558	3½*c*	....	551,558
1849	171,573	165,309	336,882	394,497	287,894	63,761	351,655	1,241,205	846,708	644,634	596,571	5*c*	....	596,571
1850	214,360	180,905	395,265	438,375	402,905	74,650	477,555	1,343,805	905,430	609,589	734,216	7*c*	....	734,216
1851	164,862	164,054	328,916	406,796	459,000	75,921	535,020	1,349,223	942,427	695,919	653,303	7*c*	....	653,303
1852	229,042	185,377½	414,419½	314,914	493,621	83,364	579,285	1,325,563	1,010,649	710,179	615.384	7*c*	....	615,384
	2,160,770	2,272,217½	4,432,997½	$3,397,942	2,838,719	940,948	3,780,467	$13,882,710	$8,470,055	$7,694,028	$6,188,679		$1,090,038	$5,098,641

a $1 cash and $2 bonds. *b* $3 in bonds. *c* Stock.

.—Commodities Transported Eastwardly from Depots on the Main Stem of the B. & O. to Baltim

21 Years—October 1, 1831, to September 30, 1852.

rticles nsported.	1832. Tons.	1833. Tons.	1834. Tons.	1835. Tons.	1836. Tons.	1837. Tons.	1838. Tons.	1839. Tons.	1840. Tons.	1841. Tons.	1842. Tons.	1843. Tons.	1844. Tons.	1845. Tons.	1846. Tons.	1847. Tons.	1848. Tons.	1849. Tons.	1850. Tons.	185 Ton
... { barrels..	146,936	169,957	182,211½	268,162	174,643	113,870	142,512¼	264,033½	392,449½	255,618	233,536	266,146½	241,550	235,602½	412,776½	579,870½	416,110½	469,261	508,127	471,8
... { tons.....	12,610	16,390	17,630	25,862	16,845	11,569	15,391	28,516	42,383	27,642	25,233	28,744	26,066	25,446	44,586*	62,599	44.717	50,007	54,636	50,9
o { hogsheads	......	631	801	2,309	2,377	2,328	1,468	861	2,115	1,367	1,884	3,456	3,598	6,670½	5,539	4,130	5,582	4,496	2,217	3,4
o { tons.......	174	351	312	898	913	908	624	368	900	572	769	1,510	1,517	2,885	2,344	1,700	2,322	1,761	876	1,2
....	353	280	523	1,500	2,348	1,848	11,106	1,263	2,004	166	255	2,508	1,878	1,923	1,172	6,693	1,475	3,347	818	4,6
tc.............	512	1,056	741	2,463	2,349	2,660	1,920	1,429	2,373	1,012	885	1,001	1,102	1,370	1,394	1.967	1.593	1,532	1,408	2,4
ons.....	29	289	161	53	354	737	647	451	414	502	201	2,870	2,403	2,352	3,192	3,824	4,705	3,808	2,121	2,2
ock	......	51	23	46	71	16	834	427	432	671	326	1,219	4,669	5,172	4,382	8,204	12.713	18,991	14,863	14,5
y	66	69	130	208	244	295	413	468	492	395	26	566	733	730	547	700	1,111	1,078	807	7
e, Lime, Soap limestone.....	8,332	13,343	10,592	8,026	9,269	10,031	7,812	4,121	5,218	4,225	3,399	2,597	4,501	5,644	5,205	6,030	6,081	4,358	5,409	6,7
....	1,574	1,143	1,548	2,523	3,796	4,833	3,269	5,006	3,030	1,024	1,389	2,485	3,552	4,810	7,543	8,855	7,326	6,722	7,556	10,9
e..............	......	......	......	......	......	......	......	......	......	......	......	......	......	......	......	......	......	3,123	2,470	4,3
d Butter	......	......	......	......	......	......	......	......	......	......	......	476	780	1,206	1,661	1,489	1,752	1,767	987	5
....	......	......	......	......	......	......	......	......	......	......	......	4,964	5,687	16,021	18,394	50,259	66,289	71,699	132,534	139,1
ood	......	......	......	......	......	......	......	......	......	......	......	......	......	......	......	......	......	91	88	6
r..............	......	......	......	......	......	......	......	......	......	......	......	......	......	......	......	......	......	696	956	1,2
....	......	......	......	......	......	......	......	......	......	......	......	......	......	......	......	......	......	1,169	559	1,1
ick	......	......	......	......	......	......	......	......	......	......	......	......	......	......	......	......	......	1,508	962	1,0
aneous........	5,766	4,194	4,562	5,400	4,616	7,799	3,647	2,803	3,257	4,273	4,133	3,964	4,219	3,502	4,250	6,136	7,861	3,353	3,288	3,7
al Tons........	29,446	37,166	36,192	46,979	40,805	40,696	45,663	44,852	60,503	40,482	36,616	52,634	57,107	71,061	94,670	158,466	157,405	175,610	230,338	245,7

* See p. 75.

5.—BIBLIOGRAPHY.

1. Annual Reports of the President of the Baltimore and Ohio Railroad Company (1827-1853).

2. Reports of the Treasurer, the Engineers, the Masters of the Road, of Machinery and of Transportation respectively, of the Baltimore and Ohio Railroad Company (1827-1853).

3. Various reports, pamphlets, broadsides, etc., etc., to be found in the library of the Maryland Historical Society of Baltimore, covering the period 1827-53.

4. Contemporary files of the Baltimore American and Daily Commercial Advertiser (1827-1853).

5. Scharf's History of Maryland. 3 vols. Baltimore, 1879.

6. Niles' Weekly Register (1826-1836).

7. "The Book of the Great Railway Celebrations of 1857." W. P. Smith. New York, 1858.

8. "Railroads: their Origin and Problems." Charles Francis Adams, Jr. New York, 1878.

9. "Bibliography of the Baltimore and Ohio Railroad Company, 1827-1879." John W. M. Lee. Baltimore, 1879.

10. "A History and Description of the Baltimore and Ohio Railroad," etc. [W. P. Smith.] Baltimore, 1853.

11. "The History of the First Locomotives in America." William H. Brown. New York, 1871.

12. "Laws and Ordinances relating to the Baltimore and Ohio Railroad Company." J. Murphy & Co., Publishers, Baltimore, 1850.

13. "History of Cumberland." W. H. Lowdermilk. Washington, 1878.

14. "The History of Western Maryland." J. T. Scharf. 2 vols.

15. "Industrial Resources of the South and West." J. B. De Bow. 3 vols. New Orleans, 1852-53.